D0621163

NOUS·SOMMES·PRETS

SIMON FRASER UNIVERSITY
W.A.C. BENNETT LIBRARY

REFORMERS
AND ACTIVISTS

AMERICAN INDIAN LIVES

REFORMERS AND ACTIVISTS

Nancy J. Nielsen

Facts On File, Inc.

Reformers and Activists

Facts On File, Inc.
11 Penn Plaza
New York NY 10001

Library of Congress Cataloging-in-Publication Data

Nielsen, Nancy J.
Reformers and activists / Nancy J. Nielsen.
p. cm.—(American Indian lives)
Includes bibliographical references and index.
ISBN 0-8160-3440-0
1. Indian activists—North America—Biography. 2. Social reformers—North America—Biography. 3. Indians of North America—Politics and government. 4. Indians of North America—Civil rights. I. Title. II. Series: American Indian lives (New York, N.Y.)
E89.N53 1997
973'.0497'00922—dc20
[B]   96-41254

Facts On File books are available at special discounts when purchased in bulk quantities for businesses, associations, institutions or sales promotions. Please call our Special Sales Department in New York at (212) 967-8800 or (800) 322-8755.

Text design by Cathy Rincon
Cover design by Molly Heron

Printed in the United States of America

MP FOF 10 9 8 7 6 5 4 3 2 1

This book is printed on acid-free paper.

When I first met Shirley Cain, a neighbor in south Minneapolis who is an Anishinabe attorney from the Red Lake Nation, I had no idea that American Indians who lived five minutes from my house were uncomfortable in the presence of a white person. As with many Indian families, however, it was impossible to get to know one member without getting to know the entire family. I soon found myself included in many family events.

When Shirley moved Up North to practice law, she arranged for me to be one of the "aunties" in her extended family. I am grateful for the sweetness and warmth I received from the children to whom this book is dedicated. It is my desire that they grow up with a strong sense of identity and self-esteem. To do this, they must know who they are and be proud of their people. It is for them that I wrote this book.

Vincent

Darrin

Kevin

Preston

and

Shannon

Raeanne

Janelle

Georgie

Suzie

The utmost good faith shall always be observed towards the Indians, their lands and liberty shall never be taken from them without their consent; and in their property, rights, and liberty, they shall never be invaded or disturbed, unless in just and lawful wars authorized by Congress; but laws founded in justice and humanity shall from time to time be made, for preventing wrongs being done to them, and for preserving peace and friendship with them . . .

—Northwest Ordinance
passed by the United States Congress
on July 13, 1787

CONTENTS

Acknowledgments   *ix*

Introduction   *xi*

GERTRUDE SIMMONS BONNIN (ZITKALA-SA)
Yankton Sioux Writer and Reformer,
President of the National Council of
American Indians (NCAI) (1876–1938)   *1*

CLINTON RICKARD
Tuscarora Chief and Activist,
Founder of the Indian Defense League
of America (IDLA) (1882–1971)   *13*

LADONNA HARRIS
Comanche Spokesperson and National Leader,
President of Americans for Indian Opportunity
(AIO) (1931–)   *24*

VINE DELORIA, JR.
Standing Rock Sioux Attorney, Writer,
and Reformer (1933–)   *35*

AMERICAN INDIAN MOVEMENT (AIM) LEADERS

DISSENTERS AND ACTIVISTS   47

Dennis Banks:
    Anishinabe AIM National Leader (1937–)   49
Russell Means:
    *Oglala Lakota/Yankton Dakota AIM National
      Leader (1940–)*   58
Anna Mae Pictou Aquash:
    Micmac AIM National Leader (1945–1976)   65

CARRIE DANN

Western Shoshone Land Rights Activist (1934–)   70

MAE WILSON TSO

Navajo Land Rights Activist (1937–)   78

JOHN E. ECHOHAWK

*Pawnee Attorney and Reformer,
Executive Director of the Native American Rights
Fund (NARF) (1945–)*   88

Selected Annotated Bibliography   96

Index   105

ACKNOWLEDGMENTS

With special thanks to the following persons who provided materials or information, or reviewed parts of the manuscript:

Barbara Graymont, editor of *Fighting Tuscarora*
LaDonna Harris and her daughter, Laura Harris
Vine Deloria, Jr.
Dennis Banks and his wife, Alice Lambert
Tom Arviso, editor of *Navajo Times* in Window Rock, Arizona
John E. Echohawk
Shirley Cain, Nancy Cain-Kouri, and Annie Cain

The author also wishes to thank the Minnesota Indian Women's Resource Center, the Minnesota Historical Society, and the many librarians at the Minneapolis Public Library and several of its branches for research assistance.

INTRODUCTION

Many books and textbooks end their coverage of the American Indian with the surrender of Chief Joseph of the Nez Percé in 1877 or of the Apache leader Geronimo in 1886. Or historians end with the deaths of such leaders as Black Kettle (Cheyenne, 1868), Crazy Horse (Lakota, 1877), and Sitting Bull (Dakota, 1890). These were the final events in the Indian Wars that resulted in the loss of lands and freedoms for the Indians, the time at which all Indian nations within the borders of the United States had finally been detained on reservations.

But the history of American Indian leaders does not stop there. Many Indian reformers and activists have worked hard during the 20th century to procure justice for their people, including the enforcement of treaty rights. They have both demanded enforcement of U.S. Indian policy and asked for changes in U.S. policy toward Indians. Although they have not agreed on all issues, contemporary Indian reformers and activists have all worked to generate understanding of Indian ways among non-Indians, and to create cultural pride in and improve the life of America's 2 million Indians.

To influence U.S. Indian policy, reformers and activists must be familiar with laws that affect Indians today. The United States signed about 400 treaties with Indian nations, in which it promised to protect Indian rights to their treaty land as well as supply them with food, clothing, health care, and other services in exchange for peace and cessions of vast amounts of land. Because these treaties are still in effect today, Indian nations by law hold sovereign rights to govern themselves and also are governed by federal laws (as opposed to state or local laws, unless Congress grants those rights to state or local governments). In addition, because Indian tribes and the U.S. government are in a guardian-ward relationship, much of Indian land is held in trust—or protected—by the U.S. government. The Bureau of Indian Affairs (BIA) was established to protect Indian rights; nevertheless, the U.S. broke its treaties with Indian nations. Through various governmental policies and laws, Indians lost treaty land and other rights guaranteed to them by the treaties.

At the turn of the century, a government policy of detribalization required Indians to give up their traditional ways of life. The Dawes Act of 1887, sometimes called the General Allotment Act, broke reservation land into small family plots of 180 acres, meant to break apart Indian communal life and encourage Indians to become farmers. The United States had promised in treaties to provide the Indians with farming equipment, but did not follow through; with no money or equipment, the Indian people were unable to till the fields or plant crops. Because the rest of reservation land was sold to settlers, Indians lost two-thirds of their land as a result of this act.

Religious freedom also was challenged during the detribalization era. In rulings contrary to the First Amendment, the Sioux Ghost Dance, a religious ceremony that advocated a return to traditional values, was outlawed in 1892. The government even banned the practice of all tribal religions in 1904. These rulings created factions between "traditional" Indians, who took their religion underground and continued to follow their traditional ways of life, and "progressive" Indians, who were willing to assimilate into non-Indian society. Adding to the problem was the fact that most traditional Indians were full-bloods, while progressives were often half Indian or less.

Because of the many problems facing American Indians, many Indian leaders began to work for reforms. Yankton Sioux reformer Gertrude Simmons Bonnin worked at the turn of the century to protect Indian land. Bonnin also worked to procure citizenship for American Indians. This was finally granted in 1924, despite the opposition of another Indian leader, Tuscarora chief Clinton Rickard, who believed Indians should retain citizenship in their own tribes alone. Rickard also worked for recognition of treaty rights that allowed Indians to pass unrestricted to and from the United States and Canada.

The Dawes Act was finally superseded in 1934 by the Indian Reorganization Act (IRA), which lifted the ban on tribal religions, supported traditional Indian culture, and encouraged greater Indian control over tribal affairs. But the act also created a charter form of government, thus imposing the government's value system upon tribes. And, despite the IRA, many Indian children continued to be forceably removed from their families and sent to boarding schools to be educated and socialized into America's "melting pot." The schools, run either by the BIA or by church groups, strictly forbade their students to follow Indian culture or religion, or even speak their own languages, under threat of corporal punishment. After schooling, students often did not fit into life either on the reservations or within the dominant society. The result of this policy was lack of identity and low self-esteem among Indians, the loss of many Indian traditions, and a breakdown of positive family values such as shared parenting.

In 1953, "termination," or forced assimilation through the abolishment of reservations and tribal sovereignty, became the official U.S. policy. Its purpose was to end trust arrangements and government support and protection for tribes. In 1953, one of the first tribes to be terminated was the Menominee of Wisconsin, who were operating a successful lumber business at the time. The result of termination, however, was a worsening of poverty, unemployment, and decent health care. Because the people were unable to pay their taxes, many had to sell their homes and farms and go on welfare, costing the government much more than they had before termination. Through the work of Menominee reformer Ada Deer, the Menominee Restoration Act was passed by Congress in 1973, restoring the tribe's status and treaty rights.

During this same period, many groups of Indians organized to work for greater control over Indian affairs. President Richard Nixon embraced the idea of Indian self-determination in 1970, leading to greater self-government by tribes. One of the first gains was the return of Blue Lake to the Taos Pueblo in New Mexico. Assisting the Taos in their fight was Comanche LaDonna Harris, president of Americans for Indian Opportunity (AIO), a Washington-based organization. Representing the tribe was Pawnee John Echohawk and other attorneys from the Native American Rights Fund (NARF). Passage of the Indian Self-Determination and Education Act followed in 1975.

During the late 1960s and early 1970s, Standing Rock Sioux attorney Vine Deloria, Jr., added his voice to the growing number of Indian reformers and activists by writing several books. *Custer Died for Your Sins*, an Indian manifesto, declared that Indians and their traditional cultures were not going away. *We Talk, You Listen* became known as "an American Indian Declaration of Independence."

The 1960s was marked by the civil rights movement in the South, the anti–Vietnam War movement, and the advent of such militant groups as the Black Panthers and the Weathermen. Struggle for land and other treaty rights led to the formation of Indian protest groups as well. As early as 1964, Indians in Washington and Oregon under the leadership of Assiniboine/Sioux Hank Adams conducted "fish-ins" to claim their fishing rights. In 1969, the National Indian Youth Council protested an annual event in Gallup, New Mexico, at which leaders bragged about being the Indian capital of the world, while excluding Indians from civic events. Also in 1969, a San Francisco Indian group seized and occupied for one and one-half years the abandoned prison on Alcatraz Island.

The best-known Indian activist organization of the 1970s is the American Indian Movement (AIM), which, under the direction of Anishinabe Dennis Banks and Lakota/Dakota Russell Means, occupied Wounded Knee, a trading post on the Pine Ridge Indian Reservation in South Dakota, declaring themselves to be the Independent Oglala Nation. They received national media coverage—some of it was supportive, while other coverage referred to them as "radicals" and "revolutionaries." Articles in *Newsweek* magazine were particularly insulting. In an attempt to be amus-

AIM cofounder Clyde Bellecourt wears a stolen tribal police jacket during the occupation at Wounded Knee, South Dakota, in 1973. (© Kevin McKiernan)

ing, they reinforced negative and offensive Hollywood movie stereotypes, referring to AIM as "redskins" and a "war party," even calling members "assorted braves and squaws."

Resistance to AIM activities by Sioux tribal president Richard Wilson and his supporters led to a "reign of terror" on the Pine Ridge Reservation, during which more than 60 AIM members and sympathizers, including Micmac Anna Mae Aquash, were murdered. In addition, many AIM members, including Dennis Banks and Russell Means, were arrested and tried for crimes that included the use of firearms, rioting, and obstruction of justice. In most cases, charges against them were dropped, or they were acquitted.

Although many people disagreed with AIM's militancy, because they received a great deal of publicity, AIM did have an effect nationwide. Interest in native religions and customs surged; in 1972, 75 books on American Indians were released. (These books, however, focused on Native America's past and ignored their contemporary conditions.)

Because AIM leaders insisted on a return to the traditional names of their tribes, people began hearing the terms *Dakota* and *Lakota* for those whom they had previously known as Sioux, a French version of a pejorative Chippewa word. Many Chippewa or Ojibwa (also pejorative terms) began to refer to themselves as Anishinabe. The Navajo returned to the traditional term Dineh; Western Shoshone resurrected the term Newe. (In this book, Indian leaders' tribal affiliations are named according to the leader's preference. If not known, the registered or legal name of the tribe is used.)

The voices of Indian reformers and activists continued to be heard. In 1973, Western Shoshone sisters in Nevada, Mary and Carrie Dann, decided not to renew a Bureau of Land Management (BLM) grazing permit for their stock as, according to treaty, the land belonged to their nation. In 1977, Mae Wilson Tso, along with several other Navajo grandmothers, began protesting the BIA's plan to turn their traditional lands over to the Hopis.

As a result of the Indian tumult of the 1970s, the American Indian Policy Review Commission Resolution was formed by

Congress to study Indian issues. In 1978, the Indian Child Welfare Act, which involved tribes in all Indian children placement decisions, and the American Indian Religious Freedom Act (AIRFA) were passed by Congress. When John Echohawk and many others realized in the 1980s that AIRFA provided insufficient protection for Indian religious freedom, they sought support for stronger congressional protections through amendments to AIRFA. Echohawk and NARF also represent many Indian tribes in the 1990s as they endeavor to hold onto their powers as sovereign nations.

The handful of leaders covered in this book is in no way inclusive of all Indian reformers and activists. Others include Frank Little (Cherokee labor organizer), Lucy Covington (Colville leader against tribal termination), Carlos Montezuma (Yavapi reformer), Hank Adams (Assiniboine/Sioux intellectual who led

AIM leaders Russell Means (left) and Pedro Bissonnette (right) are joined by Oglala Lakota holy man Wallace Black Elk during negotiations with the U.S. government at Wounded Knee in 1973. (© Kevin McKiernan)

the struggle for fishing rights in the Puget Sound area), Winona LaDuke (Anishinabe writer and activist), Ward Churchill (Creek/Cherokee Metis writer and reformer), and Roberta Blackgoat (Navajo elder and land rights activist). Regrettably, many deserving AIM leaders have been omitted, including Anishinabes Clyde and Vernon Bellecourt and Leonard Peltier; Oglala Lakotas Ken Loud Hawk, Vernon Long, Pedro Bissonnette, Ellen Moves Camp, Mary Crow Dog, and Ramon Roubideaux; Ponca Carter Camp; Western Shoshone Russ Redner; Seminole/Lakota Mike Haney; Mohawk Richard Oakes; and Yakima/Cherokee Sid Mills.

Other reformers and activists are covered in other books in the American Indian Lives series, including, in *Scholars, Writers, and Professionals*, Paiute Sarah Winnemucca, Omaha Susette LaFlesche, and Santee Sioux Charles Eastman; in *Political Leaders and Peacemakers*, Navajo Annie Dodge Wauneka and Menominee Ada Deer; and in *Performers*, Santee Sioux John Trudell. As we enter the 21st century, the list of American Indian reformers and activists continues to grow.

GERTRUDE SIMMONS BONNIN (ZITKALA-SA)

Yankton Sioux Writer and Reformer

President of the National Council of American Indians (NCAI)

(1876–1938)

As the result of a careful, first-hand investigation of Indian conditions in Eastern Oklahoma by the undersigned, it is found—

That . . . the estates of the members of the Five Civilized Tribes are being, and have been, shamelessly and openly robbed in a scientific and ruthless manner. . . .

That in many of the Counties the Indians are virtually at the mercy of groups that include the county judges, guardians, attorneys, bankers, merchants—not even overlooking the undertaker—all regarding the Indian estates as legitimate game.

—Gertrude Simmons Bonnin
(*Oklahoma's Poor Rich Indians*, 1924)

Gertrude Simmons Bonnin wrote these words as a research agent for the Indian welfare committee of the General Federation of Women's Clubs in Washington, D.C. That the federation even had an Indian welfare committee, called the Merriam Commission, also was the work of Bonnin, who as a member of the federation had pushed for its development.

An accomplished writer, orator, and musician, Bonnin nevertheless saw helping her own people as her most important work. During the early 1900s she joined with other educated Indians such as Charles Eastman and Carlos Montezuma, seeking "the advancement of the race in American enlightenment." These early reformers were the first to advocate a pantribal approach—unity among all Indian nations as they worked together for reform. Although they valued what they called a "civilized" lifestyle, they also worked for respect of Indian traditions and to free the Indians from government-imposed injustices. Their work was instrumental in setting the stage for the modern Indian reform movement.

Gertrude Simmons was born in Greenwood, Nebraska, on February 22, 1876—the same year as the Battle of Little Big Horn (where General George Custer made his "last stand"). Her father (her mother's third husband) was a white man named Felker. Her mother, Ellen Simmons, was also known by her Indian name, Tate'lyohiwin, or "Reaches for the Wind." Felker deserted the family before Gertrude was born. Because he had once offended Ellen when scolding her son, Gertrude was given that brother's last name, the last name of Ellen's second husband, John Haysting Simmons. She and her mother returned to the Yankton Agency, a section of the Great Sioux Indian Reservation just west of Yankton, South Dakota, on the Missouri River.

Gertrude remembered a carefree childhood, living in a wigwam with her mother on the banks of the Missouri River. In an article about her childhood published in 1901 in the *Atlantic Monthly*, she recalled:

Loosely clad in a slip of brown buckskin, and light-footed with a pair of soft moccasins on my feet, I was as free as the wind that blew my hair, and no less spirited than a bounding deer. These were my mother's pride—my wild freedom and overflowing spirits.

Bonnin remembered her mother as a sad and silent woman, who later explained to her daughter that her unhappiness was due to the deaths of Gertrude's uncle and half sister, who had died of illnesses after a forced march to the reservation. For this, Gertrude's mother always was bitter toward those she called "paleface," who she said "defrauded us of our land" and "forced us away."

Because her dead uncle had been a great warrior, Gertrude and her mother were treated with respect. Gertrude remembered having many guests to dinner who told her the stories of the old Indian legends. She also recalled attending public feasts and chatting with others as she accompanied her mother to fetch water from the stream. In the fall, Gertrude joined her mother and aunt to dry corn, pumpkins, berries, and plums for the winter.

Each morning Gertrude and her mother breakfasted on dried meat, unleavened bread, and strong black coffee. Then Gertrude spent the morning learning to bead. Even at a young age, she drew her own original patterns, then sewed beads onto buckskin, using sinew for thread. In the afternoons, Gertrude was free to roam in the hills. She and friends spent many happy hours digging up sweet roots to chew as gum, chasing their shadows, and playing "grown-ups."

When Gertrude was eight years old, missionaries invited her to attend a Quaker school in Wabash, Indiana. Because the missionaries told her about red apples growing on the trees and gave her a chance to ride on the "iron horse," or train, Gertrude begged her mother to let her go. Her mother hesitated, especially since Gertrude's older brother Dawee, who had attended the school for three years, said it was a difficult experience. In the end, though, Gertrude's mother sent her with the missionaries. Later in life, Gertrude reported her mother as saying: "She will need an education when she is grown, for then there will be fewer real Dakotas, and many more palefaces. This tearing her away, so young, from her mother is necessary, if I would have her an educated woman."

Wearing a buckskin dress, new moccasins, and wrapped in a blanket, Gertrude, along with seven other children from the reservation boarded the train for Indiana. She spoke no English, and recalled being troubled by the stares of the white men, women, and children on the train.

Frightened and cold, Gertrude arrived at White's Manual Institute in Wabash, Indiana, a few days later, where no one understood her language or allowed her to speak it. On the first day, Gertrude later recalled hiding under a bed so her long hair would not be cut off, for to the Sioux, short hair was worn only by mourners or cowards.

Young Gertrude's decision to go to school in the East had a strong impact on her life. By doing so, she chose the white race's education as opposed to the philosophies of Sioux leaders Sitting Bull and Crazy Horse. While some of her people were following the Ghost Dance religion, Gertrude was being educated by Catholic nuns in Indiana whose desire was to "civilize" her to become a "productive" member of society and to follow the Christian religion.

Gertrude recalled unhappy days at the school, wearing tight shoes and closely clinging dresses that Indians considered immodest, and being punished for breaking the many strict rules she did not understand. The students rose, ate, attended classes, did chores, and went to bed, all to the ringing of bells. During class one day, students were shown a picture of "the white man's devil," which so scared Gertrude that she sneaked into the room later and scratched out the devil's eyes with her pencil. But the greatest injustice, according to Gertrude, was the neglect of children by caretakers who were so busy enforcing the rules that they did not have time to notice whether or not the children under their care were sick. These experiences deeply affected Gertrude and directly led to her later attempts to explain Indian culture to the dominant society through her writing.

After three years at the school, Gertrude returned to the reservation, where she lived and attended school for the next four years. She was 14 years old when in 1890, a small group of Ghost Dancers, unarmed and starving, were slaughtered by government troops at Wounded Knee, South Dakota. Gertrude recalls feeling chaotic inside, as if she didn't belong anywhere. In her own words, she was "neither a wild Indian nor a tame one." Her education had not only caused a rift between herself and her people, but also with her mother, who no longer knew how to talk to or comfort her educated daughter.

After four years on the reservation, Gertrude attempted to escape her discomfort by returning to school in the East. After three more years at White's Manual Institute, she received a high school diploma. Against her mother's wishes, Gertrude enrolled in another Quaker school, Earlham College in Richmond, Indiana. An excellent student, Gertrude also studied music, sang in choirs, and later studied violin at the Boston Conservatory of Music. She won an oratorical contest (in which she defended Indians) at her college and second place at an intercollegiate contest held in an opera house at the state capital, during which she stated:

> What if [Indians] fought? His forests were felled; his game frightened away . . . He loved the fair land of which he was rightful owner . . . Do you wonder still that he sulked in forest gloom to avenge the desolation of his home? Is patriotism a virtue only in Saxon Hearts? . . .

Despite her achievements, Gertrude did not feel completely accepted in the white world. She had no close friends, although many of the other students, she recalls, were "courteous" to her. At the oratorical contest in the opera house, students from other colleges had objected to her presence, displaying banners that referred to her as a "squaw."

Gertrude became ill and did not complete her college education. In 1898, she accepted a teaching position at Carlisle Indian School in Carlisle, Pennsylvania. She played in the school's orchestra and went to Paris in 1900 as a chaperone, leader, and soloist. Again, she did not feel at home at the school and criticized the school for cruelties to students, including providing poor care for their illnesses.

Sent back to her reservation to recruit Indians for the school that summer, Gertrude reestablished contact with her mother and brother. She found that her brother had lost his reservation job to a white man, and that her family and many others were starving. She decided to adopt an Indian name, Zitkala-Sa, which means "Red Bird."

During her lonely evenings back at Carlisle, Zitkala-Sa began to write about her experiences, revealing the hardships that living between two worlds caused her. She also wrote down Indian

Gertrude Simmons Bonnin, 1922.   (UPI/Bettmann)

legends to share with her students. This began her lifelong tradition of using the written word as a means to accomplish her reform work and educate the public about Indian culture. At the end of the school year, she resigned her position as a teacher at Carlisle in order to study violin at the New England Conservatory of Music in Boston.

During this period Zitkala-Sa published the three-part series of articles on her life in the *Atlantic Monthly* and a collection of ancient stories called *Old Indian Legends*. She also published several short stories in *Harper's* and spoke out in favor of Indian spirituality over Christian ways in an *Atlantic Monthly* article titled "Why I Am A Pagan." Her essays and short stories often pointed out the inadequacies of off-reservation Indian schools to prepare Indians to return to their own culture. In response, the Carlisle school newspaper criticized Zitkala-Sa for "injuring herself and harming the educational work in progress for the race from which she sprang." Her emerging ideas for Indian reform were a direct challenge to the very core of Carlisle's educational policy.

Although she loved her studies and being a part of Boston's literary circles, Zitkala-Sa felt an increasing responsibility to speak up for her people. She broke off her engagement to Carlos Montezuma, a Yavapi physician whom she had met while at Carlisle, and returned to the reservation to gather material for her stories and take care of her mother.

While in South Dakota, Zitkala-Sa met another Yankton, Captain Raymond Bonnin. They married in 1902 and had a son a year later, whom they named Ohiya, meaning "Winner." Upon marrying, Zitkala-Sa returned to using the name Gertrude and was known as Gertrude Simmons Bonnin or simply Gertrude Bonnin. She was often affectionately called "Gertie" by her friends and coworkers in the reform movement.

Also in 1902, Captain Bonnin accepted a position as a school superintendent for the Bureau of Indian Affairs (BIA) on the Uintah and Ouray Reservation in Utah. Gertrude Bonnin lived there for the next 14 years, teaching school, writing, and leading a musical group. She also collaborated with William Hanson to write an Indian opera called *Sun Dance* that premiered in 1913 in Vernal, Utah. The opera was a sympathetic portrayal of Indians that explained their life and customs. The opera became quite successful and in 1937 was performed in New York City.

It was while in Utah that Bonnin first heard about the Society of American Indians (SAI), a group of educated Indians dedicated to improving conditions for their people. Although SAI members did not always agree on how to achieve this goal, they basically

---

Constitution and Laws of the Society of American Indians
Article II.—Statement of Purposes

First: To promote and co-operate with all efforts looking to the advancement of the Indian in enlightenment which leave him free as a man to develop according to the natural laws of social evolution.

Second: To provide, through our open conference, the means for a free discussion on all subjects bearing on the welfare of the race.

Third: To present in a just light a true history of the race, to preserve its records, and to emulate its distinguishing virtues.

Fourth: To promote citizenship among Indians and to obtain the rights thereof.

Fifth: To establish a legal department to investigate Indian problems, and to suggest and to obtain remedies.

Sixth: To exercise the right to oppose any movement which may be detrimental to the race.

Seventh: To direct its energies exclusively to general principles and universal interest, and not allow itself to be used for any personal or private interest.

"The honor of the race and the good of the country will always be paramount."

—Adopted in 1915

Gertrude Simmons Bonnin (third woman from right) and other repre-
sentatives of the National Council of American Indians, at the studio of
sculptor Ulric Dunbar with his statue of Sitting Bull. (UPI/Corbis-Bettmann)

favored the integration of Indians into the dominant society. The SAI also supported citizenship for Indians and opposed the work of the current BIA.

Bonnin became active in the SAI, becoming its secretary in 1916, the same year she and her husband and son moved to Washington, D.C. Although her dedication to reform was strong, she was affected by the prevalent Indian reform model of her times—assimilation. An ambivalence between assimilation and respect for Indian traditions is evident throughout her writings.

From 1916 to 1919 Bonnin edited the *American Indian Magazine,* published quarterly by the SAI. Bonnin called the magazine "A Journal of Race Progress" and offered an "open forum" where Indians and "friends of the Indian" were invited to discuss Indian issues.

Bonnin also wrote editorials for the magazine. In the spring of 1919, for example, Bonnin wrote "Black Hills Council of the Sioux," in which she pushes for the "equitable and just settlement of the Black Hills Claim," speaks out against the "Bureau System," and suggests the Indians involved in the dispute secure legal council.

In the same issue, Bonnin writes "The Ute Grazing Land," in which she patiently explains the Indian's desire to hold onto their land with "the hands of the Indian Bureau strictly off." She goes on to say that the Utes could become successful producers of the beef supply for America, as they are "natural stockmen" with a desire to engage in more extensive stock raising. If the Utes did not lose their land, "[T]hey would find at last the joy of active participation in an American enterprise," Bonnin concludes.

Through the magazine Bonnin often wrote and spoke out in favor of U.S. citizenship for Indians. She thought it deplorable for Indian soldiers to fight bravely in U.S. wars without the rights of citizenship:

> *Three-fourths of the Indian race, being non-citizen, have no legal status, though a race that is good enough to fight and die for world democracy is surely worthy of full American citizenship and the protection of law under our Constitution.*

As a member of the SAI, Bonnin also lobbied government officials on behalf of her people, lectured on Indian rights across the country, and served as SAI's representative to the BIA until the SAI was dissolved in 1920.

Shortly thereafter, Bonnin became a member of the General Federation of Women's Clubs, persuading them to establish an Indian welfare committee to look into the living conditions of Indians. As its research agent, Bonnin participated in the Oklahoma investigation during the summer of 1923 that led to writing her report, *Oklahoma's Poor Rich Indians*, revealing widespread injustice and corruption among government officials in Oklahoma.

The estates to which Bonnin referred in the report were lands granted by the government in 1901 to every Indian in Oklahoma as payment for lands previously taken from them. Although some Indians were able to keep their land, many Indians lost their estates through excess probate, administrative, and attorney fees.

Children, who also were granted 160 acres, often lost their land to white "guardians" who squandered their property, leaving nothing for them when they became of age. In some cases, guardians even allowed their wards to die of starvation.

Bonnin, along with other prominent Indian leaders, saw strong government intervention as the best solution. She concluded in her report:

> That the only hope for saving the property of the remaining . . . lies in giving to the Interior Department definite and specific authority of a character that will afford real protection to these Indians.

Bonnin went on in this report to urge all "friends of the Indians" to support a congressional bill known as S. 2313. The bill gave the Department of the Interior complete control over Indian property and Indian minors throughout the state of Oklahoma. The report was published in 1924, the same year Indians were finally granted U.S. citizenship. A few years later, President Herbert Hoover appointed two Indian rights leaders as heads of the BIA.

In 1926, Bonnin and her husband organized the National Council of American Indians (NCAI), which took the place of the SAI. The organization worked to create interest in Indian affairs and to secure recognition of personal and property rights. It was described in *The Indian's Friend* as a "non-partisan, non-sectarian organization carrying on an information service for untrained Indian citizen voters, and helping them to organize themselves in assemblies for discussion."

Bonnin served as president of the NCAI for 12 years, during which time she tirelessly traveled on national speaking tours and visited reservations to organize NCAI chapters. Bonnin and others lobbied leaders in Washington, D.C., and testified before Congress on such issues as the use of peyote, Indian education and citizenship, and land claims.

Bonnin also became involved with other Indian activist organizations, such as the Indian Rights Association of Philadelphia and John Collier's American Indian Defense Association. Collier was a leading non-Indian critic of government Indian policy, who, as head of the BIA, began an "Indian New Deal" that resulted in the

1934 passage of the Indian Reorganization Act. This led to land reclamation programs and the revitalization of tribal governments as well as a new respect for Indian culture. Although she often disagreed with Collier, Bonnin served as his advisor.

In response to criticism from Indian men for assuming a role of leadership, Bonnin also began to write about the historical role of Indian women leaders. Her work helped to prepare the way for the women Indian leaders that followed her, such as Ada Deer and LaDonna Harris.

Bonnin died on January 25, 1938, at the age of 61. She was buried in Arlington Cemetery.

CLINTON RICKARD

Tuscarora Chief and Activist

Founder of the Indian Defense League of America (IDLA)

(1882–1971)

... (L)ong before the white man came over to our country, we passed freely over this land. Now since the coming of the Europeans, a border has been set up separating Canadians and Americans, but we never believed that it was meant to separate Indians. This was our country, our continent, long before the first European set foot on it. Our Six Nations people live on both sides of this border. We are intermarried and have relatives and friends on both sides. We go back and forth to each other's ceremonies and festivals. Our people are one. It is an injustice to separate families and impose restrictions upon us, the original North Americans, who were once a free people and wish to remain free.

—Chief Clinton Rickard
(*Fighting Tuscarora*, 1971)

In 1928, people from many American Indian nations came to the first Border Crossing Celebration in Niagara Falls. They brought sled dogs, birch-bark canoes, moose and wolf hides, and ancient beaded wampum belts. Some of the people danced while others demonstrated a lacrosse game at a local park. Also in attendance were men of the American Legion and other veterans' groups that had supported Indians' right to cross freely between the United States and Canada without paying polls or tariffs on goods according to the Jay Treaty of 1794.

Honored at this celebration was Tuscarora chief Clinton Rickard along with his Indian Defense League of America (IDLA), which had successfully lobbied for the passage of border crossing legislation. Each year until his death in 1971, Chief Rickard wore Indian regalia representing several cultural traditions. His fringed moose-hide suit made by an Algonquin woman had been tanned in the traditional Indian way. The beadwork on his jacket showed a red hand symbolizing Native Americans and a white hand symbolizing European settlers, both holding a chain of friendship. The beadwork also included six stars representing the Six Nations Confederacy, and an eagle and thirteen stars representing friendship with the thirteen original United States. On his head Rickard wore an eagle-feather Plains headdress instead of the simpler Iroquois headdress.

A traditional, rather than progressive, leader, Rickard was sometimes accused of being old-fashioned and against change. But this man worked hard for peace among all people, was befriended by many white people, and fought bravely in the Spanish-American War. Throughout his long life, in which he experienced both invigorating victories and crushing defeats, Rickard continued the work of Indian reform.

The Tuscarora people are a part of a confederacy between Indian tribes of the Northeast known as the Six Nations Confederacy, or Iroquois. (The other five nations are the Mohawks, Oneidas, Onondagas, Cayugas, and Senecas.) Five or six centuries ago, the Tuscarora separated from the other nations and traveled south to what is now South Carolina. When English settlers fought them for that land during the late 1600s, however, the Tuscaroras returned to the North and eventually settled on land near Niagara Falls, given to them by the Senecas. This land eventually became the Tuscarora Reservation in the state of New York.

Clinton Rickard was born on this reservation on May 19, 1882. He was the third of four sons born to George and Lucy Rickard. His father's father, a German, had deserted his family. His father's mother, however, became a beloved grandmother, who often stayed with the family, bringing her milk cows with her. Clinton's maternal grandfather, a member of the Beaver clan, had once left for Kansas, believing the government's promise of good farmland. When the promise turned out to be false, William Garlow was lucky to be able to return to the reservation—many of the migrants died en route. Grandfather Garlow also often lived with the family. Since Tuscarora traditionally inherit the clan of their mothers, Rickard became a member of the Beaver clan.

When Clinton was four years old, his father left the family and became a member of the Wild West show, traveling to England with Buffalo Bill Cody. The family was very poor, and sometimes the boys did not have enough to eat. Clinton remembers eating lots of corn bread and cooked greens, which he remembered as being tasty.

A couple of years later, Clinton's father returned to the family. Unfortunately, George Rickard was an alcoholic and, when drinking, he was a violent man. Clinton remembered his father beating his mother and the children, Clinton included. In his autobiography, *Fighting Tuscarora*, Clinton recalled a winter night when he and his brothers hid in the outhouse and then in the bushes because his father was shooting a gun at them.

This incident and others like it led Clinton to decide at a young age to avoid alcohol. He said he went into the woods and prayed to the Great Spirit for help with three things: that he would not drink alcohol, that he would never harm a woman, and that in the future he would be allowed to protect people who were being harmed. According to Rickard, his prayers were answered.

Clinton and his family lived on a farm, and as they got older, the boys took care of cows and chickens. They plowed the fields with oxen and horses. The boys also enjoyed hunting and fishing in the reservation's woods. Later, Clinton and some of his brothers worked at a local lumber mill.

Schooling on the reservation was limited to grades one through six. Clinton attended school sporadically until he was 16 years old, but only received a third-grade education. He and his brothers walked the three miles back and forth to school, even in winter.

In 1901, when he was 18 years old, Rickard joined the U.S. Army and fought in the Philippines during the Spanish-American War. He saw the army as a chance to escape from his abusive father. He also was proud to be able to follow in the tradition of his ancestors, who had always fought as allies of the United States. After training at forts in New York, Virginia, and Vermont, Rickard was sent by ship to the Philippine Islands. On the way, the ship stopped at ports in Europe, Africa, and Asia. He arrived in Manila on February 3, 1902.

Rickard was the only Indian in his brigade. Affectionately called "Chief" by the other men, he fought hard and distinguished himself as a soldier during the next three years. One of his greatest feats was a climb up Mt. Banahao to conquer an enemy stronghold in a crater. Rickard was a large, strong man who often found himself carrying arms for comrades who were too exhausted to carry the guns themselves. He also saved his captain's life during battle. Even after a serious bout with malaria, Rickard continued to serve. He received an honorable discharge as a qualified marksman with excellent character.

Rickard promptly reenlisted in the army, but on a vacation leave to the Tuscarora reservation, he fell in love with a woman named Ivy. He requested a discharge from the army and returned to the reservation to marry. Although he still suffered recurring attacks of malaria, Rickard took a job working for a farmer who lived near the reservation. Later, he worked for the Empire Limestone Quarry. The couple had two children, Edith and Herald.

In 1912, Ivy became ill and took the children to stay with relatives in Oklahoma, believing she would do better in a dry climate. On February 25, 1913, she died. One month later, their son Herald died from whooping cough. Rickard traveled to Oklahoma for each funeral. He then left Edith in Oklahoma with her grandmother. Disaster struck again when Rickard was caught in the great 1913 flood in Waverly, Iowa, on the way home, and lost all of his possessions.

Heartbroken, Rickard returned to the reservation and his job at the quarry. That fall, his boss invited him to join the Masonic Lodge, a fraternal organization that promotes brotherhood and morality. Being a Freemason had been an ambition of Rickard's since he was a young boy. Rickard became a Mason and remained one the rest of his life, receiving all of the Masonry degrees. His involvement helped him slowly recover from his grief for his wife and son.

Clinton Rickard prepares his sons Clark (left, age 9) and William (right, age 12) to participate in a junior crossbow tournament in 1931. (Buffalo and Erie County Historical Society)

Three years later, Rickard married another woman, Elizabeth Patterson, with whom he had two sons, William and Clark. A third son, Ralph, was born in 1923 and died shortly after birth. Rickard's daughter Edith also returned to live with them on the reservation.

By now, Rickard was farming full-time. He grew vegetables and Indian corn, using a team of oxen to plow the fields. The family also raised milk cows, chickens, and ducks, and tended several orchards. In the spring, they collected sap from trees and made syrup and sugar. These foods, along with fish caught in the streams, supplied nearly all the food they needed.

During the 1920s, Rickard became a chief, representing his clan at the Chiefs' Council. The Council during these years succeeded in building a gymnasium on the reservation and dealt with such problems as non-Indians coming onto reservation land to cut timber. Rickard supported traditional government and worked in opposition to "progressive" chiefs who wanted to bring about change. He especially fought Chief Grant Mt. Pleasant, whom Rickard said was greedy for land and accumulated it in illegal ways. In 1925, Rickard was elected treasurer of the Chiefs' Council. In 1930, he became the Council's president and was successful in securing increased state funding for Indian schools on reservations and for Indians to attend public high schools in nearby towns.

Rickard increasingly became involved in Indian rights. He served as a Tuscarora delegate for the Everett Report, which demonstrated to the State of New York how the Six Nations had been swindled out of 18 million acres of land. Rickard also (unlike Sioux reformer Gertrude Simmons Bonnin) fought against citizenship being forced on Indians. As he said in his autobiography:

> We had our own citizenship. We did not want or need the white man's type of citizenship . . . How can a citizen have a treaty with his own government? To us, it seemed that the United States government was just trying to . . . make us into taxpaying citizens who could sell their homelands and finally end up in the city slums.

Commenting on the passage of the 1924 Citizenship Act, which made all Indians U.S. citizens, Rickard stated: "This was a violation of our sovereignty. Our citizenship was in our own nations. We had a great attachment to our style of government. We wished to remain treaty Indians and preserve our ancient rights."

The passage of both the Citizenship Act and the Immigration Act in 1924 led to a three-year fight to keep the U.S.–Canadian border open for Indians. The Immigration Act stated that "No alien ineligible for citizenship shall be admitted to the United States." Canadian Indians were not eligible for U.S. citizenship. Yet many Indians in Canada had relatives living across the border in the U.S., and vice versa. They were used to crossing over the border to visit each other.

Rickard was at this time supporting the Indian rights work of Deskaheh, a Six Nations leading chief from Canada, with whom he shared similar views. Problems at the border complicated their work. When Deskaheh stayed at the Rickard farm to keep certain speaking engagements, for example, Rickard began to get letters from Deskaheh's family and supporters who had been barred from crossing into the United States.

Rickard began to write letters of protest to the Bureau of Immigration and other departments, asking that the Jay Treaty of 1794 be upheld. This treaty between the United States and Great Britain had given Indians the right to cross the border with their own goods at any time. The Treaty of Ghent, which had ended the War of 1812, also upheld this right for Indians. Rickard became totally dedicated to this cause, even neglecting his farm work to write letters and visit government officials.

In 1925, Rickard scored a partial victory when the U.S. Department of Labor stated that Indians could cross the border for short periods of time, but problems with crossing continued. An Indian man born in Canada, for example, had married a Tuscarora woman and had lived on the Tuscarora reservation for years. Yet he was denied readmittance to the United States when returning from a visit to Canada. Other Indians were jailed for several months while "waiting deportation" or because they could not pay the $8 a head tax for crossing.

To better organize for border-crossing rights, Rickard and others started an organization in 1926 called the Six Nations Defense

League. Later they changed the name to the Indian Defense League of America (IDLA) and worked for Indian border crossing and other rights nationwide. Rickard began to travel and speak on Indian rights for the league, and continued his letter-writing campaign. Rickard also began to testify at the trials of Indians who were arrested for illegal entry into the United States.

His work took Rickard several times to Washington, D.C., where he lobbied members of Congress and testified before committees on behalf of border-crossing rights. In 1927, 11 bills were introduced to Congress favoring free crossing for Indians. All were similar to H.R. 11351, which stated:

> *That the Immigration Act of 1924 shall not be construed to apply to the right of American Indians born in Canada to pass the borders of the United States: Provided, that this right shall not extend to persons whose membership in Indian tribes or families is created by adoption.*

This bill was passed by the Senate on March 21, 1928, and by the House on March 29. It was signed into law by President Calvin Coolidge on April 2, 1928. Rickard heard the news from his wife, who heard it on the radio. He immediately began planning for a Border Crossing Celebration in Niagara Falls, which has turned into a permanent annual event.

This great success, however, was marred by divisions among people on the reservation. Other chiefs on the Tuscarora Reservation were against the free border crossing, complaining that the "Canadian Indians" were "squatting" on their land. Tension was so high that Rickard's son William was taunted at school for his father's actions. One day, William received a severe beating by schoolmates from which he never completely recovered. He was left with a constricted chest that would cause lung problems for the rest of his life.

Then, less than a year after the border-crossing victory, Rickard's second wife, Elizabeth, died in childbirth. She had been a great companion in the fight for border-crossing rights, and her death plunged Rickard into despair. Their newborn son, Eli, was given to Elizabeth's sister, Nellie, to raise.

Chief Clinton Rickard, 1947. (Buffalo and Erie County Historical Society)

Rickard consoled himself by working on the claim of the Cayugas, a Six Nations tribe in Canada that had lost land to New York state in the late 1700s. Although Cayugas living in the United States received an annuity from the state of New York, Cayugas in Canada did not. In 1925, Canada supported the Cayugas and demanded that the United States pay them as well for the loss of land, but still nothing happened. Finally, Rickard in 1929 procured an interview with the then-governor of New York, Franklin D. Roosevelt, bringing along a copy of the 1795 Treaty of Cayuga Ferry. As a result of this meeting, New York awarded the Cayugas $100,000.

After this victory, Rickard again suffered another setback. In September 1931, he was jailed in Canada for allegedly raising money contrary to Canada's Indian Act. While he spent only 10 days in jail, Rickard was forced to turn his life savings over to his attorney. He later claimed he was also given poisoned soup that caused a paralytic seizure and led to a permanent decline in his health.

Newly married to his third wife, Beulah, Rickard returned to the farm. The Rickards were penniless, and the Great Depression had just begun. With no money, Rickard could not afford the seeds and horses needed for farming. He was unable to find a job because whites, he said, were always hired first. Yet according to the state of New York, he could not collect welfare because he lived on the reservation. He and his third wife had seven children together. Their oldest son, Charles, was killed in a hunting accident in 1945.

Believing that Indians fared better under federal laws, Rickard preferred working directly with the federal government on Indian matters. He fought strongly against the Snell Bill, introduced to Congress in 1931, which would turn control of reservations in New York to the state. He was still fighting against this in 1948 when the policy of termination (loss of federal recognition of Indian tribes) was first favored by President Harry Truman.

Rickard lost the battle against state control. In 1949, New York's federal Indian office was closed. Rickard and the IDLA worked hard against termination, however, and the Six Nations were never terminated under that policy.

Rickard fought his last major battle during the late 1950s against New York's State Power Authority (SPA) in its attempt to build a dam that would turn part of the Tuscarora Reservation land into a reservoir. In 1957, the SPA claimed 1,383 acres, one-fifth of the reservation land. When SPA officials came onto reservation land to begin surveying, Rickard and others met them with barricades and warning notices against trespassing. Although the SPA offered them money for their land, the Tuscarora made it clear their land was not for sale. The conflict eventually resulted in the arrest of several demonstrators, including William, Rickard's son.

Although Rickard and the reservation were able to get several restraining orders against the SPA and their case was eventually heard in the United States Supreme Court, in 1960 the reservation lost their land to the electric company. In his autobiography, Rickard claims that a dam built to form the reservoir caused the death of fish, and in turn fishing, on the reservation.

Throughout the 1960s, Rickard continued to work for reform. He supported the Seneca Nation in their fight to block the building of the Kinzua Dam, which flooded their reservations. He worked, he says in his autobiography, to warn Indians of "shyster lawyers" who would try to gain their confidence only to rob them of funds. By now, Rickard was a well-known Indian leader, and many Indians including Hopi and Shoshone traveled to his reservation to visit him.

Rickard also began to meet with Barbara Graymont, head of the department of History and Economics at Nyack College in Nyack, New York. Graymont was interested in preserving the Tuscarora language. Later, she began to help Rickard record his autobiography. Through the illnesses of his last years, Rickard continued to work with Graymont on what he called "the history book." After he died on June 14, 1971, the book was published with Graymont as its editor. It ends with this statement from Rickard, a goal for which he worked all of his life: "My experience through more than eighty years has taught me that people of good will of all races can work together to bring about justice for all and the betterment of mankind. May the Great Spirit help us all."

LADONNA HARRIS

Comanche Spokesperson
and National Leader

President of
Americans for
Indian Opportunity (AIO)

(1931–)

There is no "Indian problem" or "Black problem." There
is an American problem, a human problem, a problem
of making clear that the right to be different and still
entitled to full citizenship must be not only safeguarded
but also encouraged.

—LaDonna Harris
(*Redbook*, February 1970)

In 1995, at the age of 64, Comanche LaDonna Harris reflected over
four decades of work for Indian rights. When asked to name her
greatest accomplishment, Harris replied, "Without a doubt, testi-
fying before the Senate regarding the Taos Blue Lake issue."

Blue Lake and its surrounding area near Taos, New Mexico, is sacred to the Taos Indians, a place where Taos Pueblo rituals and ceremonies have taken place for centuries. Federal officials, however, included Blue Lake within the boundaries of the Carson National Forest when they established it in 1906. Ever since, Taos Indians had worked diligently to bring the sacred lake back within reservation boundaries and their control.

In the late 1960s, this issue finally reached lawmakers in Washington, D.C. LaDonna Harris was at that time a member of the National Council for Indian Opportunity (NCIO), and she strongly supported the Taos Indians. In 1969, she used her influence to make sure the issue was included in a NCIO report on the current state of Indian affairs. Harris also tirelessly lobbied members of Congress and was instrumental in securing support for the bill from a conservative Republican White House under President Richard Nixon. Finally, Harris was able to testify on the Taos Pueblo's behalf at a Senate hearing in 1970. Through her hard work and the work of her husband (a U.S. senator) and other leaders, Congress voted in December of 1970 to return the sacred lake to the Taos Pueblo.

LaDonna Harris was able to offer invaluable support for the Blue Lake bill because she was in a prominent position, as an Indian member of a national council whose purpose was to advise the country's leaders on Indian affairs, at an opportune time. She is a dedicated, energetic woman who has made building bridges between Tribal America and the dominant society her life's mission. This strong Comanche leader has lived—and thrived—among diverse cultures. She was born to a Comanche mother and an Irish-American father. A blue-eyed, light-haired girl, she was raised by her Comanche grandfather, an Eagle medicine man, and her Comanche grandmother, a devout Christian. LaDonna married a white man, and gave her children both Comanche and English names. And although she grew up in the wilds of rural Oklahoma, LaDonna Harris fought for Indian rights in the political citadel of America, Washington, D.C.

Lily Tabbytite was a young Comanche woman in 1930 when she married Don Crawford. Although the marriage did not last, they had one child, LaDonna, born on February 15, 1931, in Temple, Oklahoma. An interracial marriage was uncommon in Oklahoma in the 1930s, and the couple was subjected to hostility from neighbors. Perhaps for this reason, Don Crawford left his family and Oklahoma for good. Although he sent letters from his new home in California, he never returned. Lily took a job as a resident dietitian at the Indian Hospital in Lawton, Oklahoma. LaDonna went to live with Lily's parents on a farm near the small town of Walters, Oklahoma.

LaDonna's grandparents had grown up on the Kiowa-Comanche-Apache Reservation in southwest Oklahoma. Her grandfather, Tabbytite, was sent as a young boy to a government boarding school. When school officials tried to get him to give up Comanche ways and cut off his long braids, though, he ran away. Later Tabbytite worked as a cowhand in northern Texas. In 1892, he served in Indian Troop L of the U.S. Cavalry, at Fort Sill. Along with other members of his family, Tabbytite wisely selected fertile land for farming in Cotton County when, in 1901, the government awarded 160 acres of land to every Comanche man, woman, and child as payment for land taken.

Although LaDonna lived with her grandparents during the Great Depression, she was happy and well provided for on the farm. She and her aunt, Rose Marie, who was only eight months older than LaDonna, played in the orchards and pecan groves, rode horses bareback in the open fields, and floated on logs in Cache Creek. In the evening, the two girls gathered eggs, watered plants, and did other farm chores.

The Tabbytites were a large, warm, and caring extended family that included many aunts, uncles, and cousins. The family often gathered together for fun, and relatives were there to help each other when needs arose. LaDonna recalls that, according to Comanche tradition, the children were not physically punished:

What kept us in line was the importance of winning the approval and praise of the family, because if we did something silly, the teasing and joking about it could be unbearable.

If we were really out of line, we were simply ignored, and that was worse than any other type of punishment. If other discipline was needed, one of our aunts or older cousins was called in, because in the Indian way, parents are more for loving than for scolding or punishing.

Grandfather Tabbytite was a medicine man. He and his wife, Wick-kie, wore traditional dress and spoke only the Comanche language. He used peyote, a sacred plant that, when consumed during religious ceremonies, was believed to lead to a heightened spiritual experience. LaDonna remembers being healed through one of her grandfather's ceremonies when she became sick. Tabbytite also ran a successful farm that gained him respect with the local white community. He also owned the first automobile in Cotton County.

When LaDonna and Rose Marie were sent to the public school in Temple, they spoke only Comanche. Grandmother Wick-kie did not send them to the Indian boarding school because she did not want them to be homesick, as LaDonna's mother had been. Wick-kie also felt that the girls needed an education that would prepare them to live with an understanding of the whole community, both Indian and non-Indian. After all, she reasoned, this was the world in which the girls would live.

It wasn't until she attended school that LaDonna encountered racism. The jeers and insults of some of the children on the bus embarrassed and confused her. Even so, LaDonna thinks she was more fortunate than other Indian children at the school who came from impoverished homes.

It took me longer to begin to feel that I was "different," and therefore somehow inferior to non-Indian children. But gradually I got the message too—through the subtle downgrading that was constantly taking place and the general atmosphere of prejudice that chips away at the self-esteem of Indian children.

LaDonna began dating her future husband, schoolmate Fred Harris, when she was 16 years old. She was boarding with a family in Walters at that time, because no bus service was available, and LaDonna's grandmother wanted her to be able to participate in after-school activities. LaDonna also held her first job, as a waitress at a soda fountain, to help pay her expenses. She graduated from Walters High School in 1949.

Fred was the son of poor sharecroppers. He learned to speak Comanche from LaDonna, and often visited the Tabbytite farm. Together he and LaDonna attended the Indian Baptist Church with Grandmother Wick-kie. Fred was 19 years old and LaDonna was 18 when they married and moved into a trailer house in Norman, Oklahoma. A year later, their daughter Kathryn was born. In 1957, son Byron was born, and in 1961, daughter Laura was born.

From the beginning, the marriage was a partnership of common struggle and commitment. Fred was a brilliant student who worked hard to put himself through college. LaDonna earned extra money as a child care provider, and later she took a job in the University of Oklahoma library. Fred graduated in 1952 with a degree in political science and history, then attended law school. After he graduated first in his class, the Harrises moved to Lawton, Oklahoma, where Fred established a successful law firm. In 1956, at the age of 25, Fred was elected to the Oklahoma state senate.

While caring for her family and campaigning for her husband, LaDonna became more and more concerned about Indian rights. She was a part of a movement to integrate the all-white town of Lawton. Her special concerns, however, were economic opportunity and education for Indians. Appointed to the board of the Southwest Center for Human Relations Studies of the University of Oklahoma in 1963, Harris convinced them to set up an Indian education project. The program included career conferences, counseling, and later, courses in leadership training for Indian students.

In 1964, Fred Harris began the first of eight years as a U.S. senator, and the family moved to Washington, D.C. LaDonna Harris, however, continued her activism in the state of Oklahoma through multiple flights between the two locations. In 1965, Harris helped to organize a statewide meeting of Indians to discuss their problems and talk about possible solutions. From this meeting Oklahomans for Indian Opportunity was born, and

LaDonna Harris.

Harris became its president. The organization is still a vital force in Oklahoma.

Also in 1965, the Harris family traveled in Argentina, Brazil, Chile, and Peru to represent the United States. While in these countries, LaDonna Harris visited as many Indian communities as she could. She also became interested in the work of the Peace Corps, a U.S. volunteer organization.

After returning to the United States, Harris persuaded the Peace Corps to establish an Indian-to-Indian exchange between Indians in the United States and in South America. Called the Peace Pipe Project, it sent Indian Peace Corps volunteers to work with Latin American Indians.

Harris's husband also was a strong supporter of Indian rights. In a meeting with Secretary of the Interior Stewart Udall at their Washington home in 1968, the Harrises recommended the establishment of a cabinet council devoted to tribal issues. After President Lyndon B. Johnson established the National Council for Indian Opportunity (NCIO), he appointed LaDonna Harris to be one of its Indian members.

During the Nixon administration, which began in 1969, however, Harris became frustrated with the inaction of the council. Vice President Spiro Agnew had assumed chairmanship and had called only one meeting, scheduled for January of 1970. Harris continued the council's work on her own by lobbying for the Blue Lake bill as well as by holding public hearings on conditions of Indian life in Los Angeles, Minneapolis, Dallas-Ft. Worth, and San Francisco.

Because of her work, Harris knew only too well the problems facing what she calls Tribal America. She began to speak out against the "slow, ineffective, and paternalistic" handling of Indian problems by the Bureau of Indian Affairs (BIA). "Instead of helping the Indian to become strong and self-sufficient, the tendency has been to make him helpless and dependent," she said, emphasizing, "It's high time this country did something decisive for Indian-American citizens."

Harris's words brought her national attention. In 1969, a Washington newspaper reported that a "war" might begin between "the Comanches" and Agnew. The media attention gave Harris even more opportunity to speak out for American Indians. In 1970, *Redbook* published a feature story about the strong Comanche leader.

It was during this time that Harris worked for the return of Blue Lake to the Taos Pueblo. The victory was the first large land settlement ever won by Indians and the first based on religious freedom. The day the bill was signed into law was "a beautiful day," Harris recalls:

Unlike any other signing that anybody had ever been to . . . There was a different satisfaction than [with] any piece of legislation that people had been involved in . . . There was such a human element and the [Taos] people showed that they were so directly affected by the return [of Blue Lake] as to who they were and how they saw themselves continuing that it captured everyone . . .

Harris's impatience with the National Council for Indian Opportunity led her to start her own organization, Americans for Indian Opportunity (AIO), patterned after her successful Oklahomans for Indian Opportunity. Founded in 1970, the purpose of the AIO was to develop new opportunities for Indian people in a changing world. Through her efforts the AIO launched projects that ranged from helping individual tribes preserve their land's environment to setting up health-care systems for Indians.

Harris built her organization on the belief that strong tribal governments are beneficial both for Tribal America and the United States. She strongly believes that tribes should be self-sufficient and determine their own futures, and her work supports tribes as sovereign and independent nations. Her influence has allowed Harris to demonstrate to government officials the integral role that tribes play in the United States, especially in the areas of environmental protection and the development of sustainable agriculture. This work has led to the adoption of official Indian policies by several federal departments, including the Environmental Protection Agency, the Department of Energy, and the Department of Agriculture.

In 1976, Harris founded another organization, Council for Energy Resource Tribes (CERT), to assist tribes in managing such resources as timber and coal on reservation land. The work of CERT not only enhanced tribal self-determination but also resulted in an improvement of the economic status of Indian tribes throughout the United States.

Throughout her long career with the AIO, Harris has held forums, spoken at many conferences, and published many papers on Indian and environmental issues. For example, she facilitated governance forums with such tribes as the Poarch Creek, Winnebago, Comanche, Cheyenne-Arapaho, Pawnee, Apache, and Menominee tribes. Afterward, Harris meticulously wrote papers on the outcome of each forum, including such titles as *Building Consensus on a Winnebago Self-Sufficiency Plan* (1987) and *Designing the Future of the Comanche Tribe* (1990).

As an influential Indian leader, Harris has offered support to other Indian organizations as well. When the American Indian Movement (AIM) staged its takeover in 1972 of the BIA headquarters in Washington, D.C., Harris spent a night with the AIM activists in the BIA headquarters, hoping her presence and influence might help to avert a clash with riot police. When *U.S. News & World Report* in April 1973 reported that the changes requested by the activists could mean a doubling of federal spending on tribal activities, Harris replied that "anything less would fall short of the goal."

Indian affairs are not Harris's only concerns. She also became involved in many feminist issues while in Washington, D.C. She was a board member of the National Organization for Women (NOW) and in 1970 participated in Ring Around the Capitol, an anti–Vietnam War demonstration led by feminists. In 1971, Harris became a founding member of the National Women's Political Caucus, and in 1974 she was named to President Gerald Ford's U.S. Commission on the Observance of International Women's Year.

Harris also worked on her husband's campaign when he ran (unsuccessfully) for the presidential nomination at the 1976

Democratic National Convention. In 1980, LaDonna Harris ran for vice president of the United States as a member of the Citizen's Party, where she added environmental issues to the platform.

Harris also became involved with the civil rights and world peace movements. She has served on the boards of the National Urban League, National Committee Against Discrimination in Housing, Save the Children's Federation, National Institute for Women of Color, Pax World Foundation, National Organization on Fetal Alcohol Syndrome, and Every Child by Two (an immunization program). She has founded other Indian organizations besides AIO and CERT, including the National Indian Housing Council and the National Indian Business Association. She has served on several presidential commissions, including the Commission on Mental Health and the United Nations Education, Science and Culture Organization (UNESCO) under President Jimmy Carter's administration, and the Institute of American Indian Arts Board under President Bill Clinton. In 1993, Harris was appointed to the National Advisory Council on Information Infrastructure.

Out of a desire to get away from the stresses and distractions of Washington, D.C., and to regain her focus in "Indian country," in 1994 Harris relocated Americans for Indian Opportunity to Bernalillo, New Mexico (on the Santa Ana Pueblo Reservation). There the AIO continues its work creating coalitions among tribes and between Indians and non-Indians. Harris also has created INDIANnet, a computer telecommunications network, because she believes learning and using computer technology is an important skill as tribes plan for the 21st century. The AIO also offers the American Indian Ambassadors program *Medicine Pathways for the Future*, an Indian leadership training program. In addition, it has expanded to work with the international community, believing that Native Americans' experiences and values have much to offer the world. Each new activity is just another step toward LaDonna Harris's lifelong dream—creating understanding and harmony between people of diverse cultures.

Awards Received by LaDonna Harris

Outstanding American Citizen, 1965

Human Rights Award: National Education Association, 1969

United Nations Peace Medal, 1976

Woman of the Year and of the Decade, *Ladies' Home Journal*, 1979

Mary Church Terrell Award for Distinguished Public Service, Delta Sigma Theta Sorority

Toast and Strawberries Salute for Community Service: Washington, D.C., Black Business Association

Award for Public Service, Theta Sigma Phi, National Journalism Fraternity for Women

Outstanding Leadership in Advancing Public Support: 1990 Census

Lucy Covington Award for a Life of Leadership, 1994

Awards of Appreciation
   Council of Energy Resource Tribes, 1986
   Indian Health Service, 1987
   Comanche Tribe, 1988
   National Council on Aging, 1988
   Environmental Protection Agency, 1991
   National Congress of American Indians, 1992
   Department of Agriculture, 1993

Honorary Degrees; University Honors
   Board of Visitors, University of Oklahoma, Norman, Oklahoma
   Board of Trustees, Antioch University, Yellow Springs, Ohio
   Honorary Doctor of Law, Dartmouth College, Hanover, New Hampshire
   Honorary Doctor of Humanities, Marymount College, Tarrytown, New York
   Honorary Doctor of Humane Letters, Cedar Crest College, Allentown, Pennsylvania
   Honorary Doctor of Public Service, Westfield State College, Westfield, Massachusetts
   Honorary Doctor of Humanities, Northern Michigan University, Marquette, Michigan

VINE DELORIA, JR.

Standing Rock Sioux
Attorney, Writer, and Reformer

(1933–)

The primary goal and need of Indians today is not for someone to feel sorry for us and claim descent from Pocahontas to make us feel better. Nor do we need to be classified as semi-white and have programs and policies made to bleach us further. Nor do we need further studies to see if we are feasible. We need a new policy by Congress acknowledging our right to live in peace, free from arbitrary harassment. We need the public at large to drop the myths in which it has clothed us for so long. We need fewer and fewer "experts" on Indians. What we need is a cultural leave-us-alone agreement, in spirit and in fact.
　　　　　　　　　　　　—Vine Deloria, Jr.
　　　　　　　　　　　　(*Custer Died for Your Sins*, 1969)

The 1960s were turbulent years in the United States, a decade of assassinations and social rebellions, including the counterculture "hippie" and anti-war movements and civil rights demonstrations. The Black Power movement was strong, but Indians were silent—until the advent of Vine Deloria's book, *Custer Died for Your Sins*, often referred to as an Indian manifesto.

The name "Custer" in the book's title refers to U.S. General George Armstrong Custer, who, along with his entire regiment, was killed by Indians at the Battle of Little Big Horn in Montana in 1876. The book's title further refers to a Judeo-Christian concept that a blood sacrifice must be made to atone, or make amends, for sin. Vine Deloria's message was that Indians and Indian culture will survive regardless of the dominant society's desire for them to assimilate.

Deloria's intelligence and forthright style made him eminently capable of writing the Indian manifesto. Throughout his life Deloria has continued to reiterate the same messages—in other books and articles of social commentary, technical law books, and through professorships at universities, and speeches.

The Deloria are prominent among the Sioux (or Dakota) in South Dakota because so many family members have excelled. Deloria's grandfather's great grandfather was a French fur trader who married a Sioux woman. His marriage into the Yankton Sioux is noted on a Yankton "Winter Count" for the year 1783. His grandson, Vine's great-grandfather, was a prominent chief and medicine man of the Yanktons. Deloria's grandfather, Tipi Sapa or Philip, was converted to Christianity and became an Episcopal priest and missionary. Vine's father, Vine Deloria, Sr., also became an Episcopal priest. His aunt, Ella Cara Deloria, was a linguist and anthropologist, and his brother is an attorney.

Vine was born in 1933 in South Dakota, where his father was the Episcopal priest at the Pine Ridge and later the Sisseton-Wahpeton reservations. Although Vine's father was a Christian, he also revered traditional Indian ways. Vine grew up listening to traditional stories about the tribe and its heroes. He listened to warriors recount their acts of bravery during the Battle of Little Big Horn. His father often pointed out people who had survived the massacre of unarmed Sioux by U.S. soldiers at Wounded Knee in 1890, explaining that all the people had an obligation to offer them support. One of his most vivid childhood memories is a trip to the site of the Wounded Knee massacre. Vine's father also showed his son the beautiful landscapes and told him stories associated with them to teach Deloria that his people cherished the land.

Vine's mother, he recalls, "pushed me to read and get an education." Vine attended Kent School, a preparatory school in Connecticut, from which he graduated in 1951. He then attended Iowa State University because his father had taken a small church in Denison, Iowa, after losing his voice on the reservation due to overwork. Interrupting his time at Iowa State, Deloria spent two years in the Marine Corps at San Diego and Quantico, Virginia.

Deloria graduated from college in 1958. He then married a Swedish woman, Barbara Nystrom. Their son Philip was born in 1959. Daniel was born in 1960, and a daughter, Jeanne, was born in 1963. Deloria attended Augustana Lutheran Seminary in Rock Island, Illinois. His father-in-law secured him a job as a welder, and Deloria spent days studying theology and nights building the front panels of International Harvester trucks. He received a master's degree in sacred theology in 1963.

After graduating, Deloria took a position in Denver with United Scholarship Service, a church-related group. His job was to visit reservations and find capable Indian high school students for secondary school placement programs. Deloria chose his students on academic performance alone, but soon found out that supporters of the fund wanted him to adopt a paternalistic approach and make exceptions to "help" Indians. Feeling that the supporters were misled, Deloria began to have his first doubts about working for the church.

A year later, Deloria accepted a position as director of the National Congress of American Indians (NCAI) in Washington, D.C. The NCAI had been established in 1944 as a representative congress of Indian leaders who met to discuss issues of national priority for Indians. During Deloria's three years as director, the NCAI fought against the termination of tribes despite threats from the BIA that their own tribes would be targeted. They helped the Tigua Indians of El Paso, Texas, obtain formal recognition as a tribe, and then located other small tribes that needed the same assistance. The NCAI under the directorship of Deloria also began a program to upgrade tribal financial independence as an antidote to poverty.

Being director of the NCAI was an eye-opener for Deloria, who learned a great deal about the complexity of Indian problems and the various solutions leaders had for resolving them. He kept very busy, traveling to meet with tribal councils and government agencies, attending conferences, raising funds, and working to affect legislation. He found that the real impact of NCAI meetings was the personal trust developed between the various tribal leaders, but became discouraged as he watched leaders being played against each other for individual financial gain.

Despite his efforts, Deloria did not feel that life for the ordinary reservation Indian was being affected that much. He decided to attend law school, convinced that a secure knowledge of the legal system would provide him with the best tools for helping his people.

Deloria returned to Denver as a programs consultant for NCAI and attended law school at the University of Colorado. It was while he was a law student that Deloria wrote and published his first book, *Custer Died for Your Sins*. The book soon became known as "the cornerstone of native resistance" and was quoted by Indian activists nationwide.

In the book he stands up for land rights, for example, by saying, "To imply that Indians were given land is to completely reverse the facts of history." Then Deloria goes on to explain that *Indian tribes gave land to the United States* in exchange for their survival as tribes.

Custer Died for Your Sins is not all serious dialogue, however. Deloria even devotes an entire chapter to Indian humor. Although the chapter is full of Indian jokes on such historical characters as Christopher Columbus and George Custer, Deloria makes it clear at the beginning of the chapter that his real purpose is to explain Indians to the dominant society:

It has always been a great disappointment to Indian people that the humorous side of Indian life has not been mentioned by professed experts on Indian affairs. Rather the image of the granite-faced grunting redskin has been perpetuated by American mythology . . . The Indian people are exactly opposite of the popular stereotype.

In a chapter devoted to missionaries, Deloria quips, "Columbus managed to combine religion and real estate in . . . claiming the new world for Catholicism and Spain." His advice to African Americans is "to survive, blacks must have a homeland where they can withdraw, drop the facade of integration, and be themselves."

Deloria also shares biting insights about American society. On violence in America, he writes, "The [United States] was founded in violence. It worships violence and it will continue to live violently." On democracy, Deloria states, "True democracy was more prevalent among Indian tribes in pre-Columbian days than it has been since." On America's future, he refers to the Golden Rule, "Do unto others as you would have them do unto you." Considering America's past, Deloria prophetically claims, its future is in peril.

Although Deloria spoke clearly and to the point, he often felt that "no one" was listening. Some of his ideas, however, did become law. In the early 1970s, President Richard Nixon reversed the policy of termination of tribes and spoke in favor of self-determination. Public Law 635 gave tribal governments responsibility for some of the functions of the Bureau of Indian Affairs (BIA). The American Indian Religious Freedom Resolution and the Indian Child Welfare Act both were passed by Congress in 1978.

Deloria published a second book, *We Talk, You Listen*, in 1970. It soon became known as "an American Indian Declaration of Independence." In it, he stated that America's "salvation" was a return to tribalism, or small groups of like-minded people who hold mutual respect for each other.

American society is undergoing a total replacement of its philosophical concepts . . . Instead of repression and conformity we should open as many options as possible to as many groups and interests as possible. By creating the most flexible situation we can, we may find the tools and techniques to survive the changes ahead.

Vine Deloria, Jr., c. 1970

When *Custer Died for Your Sins* received the Anisfield Wolf Award in 1970 and *We Talk, You Listen* was awarded a special citation by the National Conference of Christian and Jews, Deloria began to receive national recognition as a spokesperson for Indians.

Deloria received a law degree in 1970, moved his family to Washington State, and became involved with the Indian fishing-rights controversy in that area. When Deloria was a guest on the Dick Cavett show that same year, he brought along pictures of the brutality police displayed against the Puyallup and Nisqually fishing camp near Tacoma, Washington. Soon after the pictures were shown on national television, the Justice Department filed suit in federal court against the state of Washington, seeking to defend the treaty, in which Indians clearly retained the rights to fish. In 1974, the Supreme Court upheld the treaty, resulting in a legally established right of the Indian tribes of that state to half of the annual catch of salmon.

While in Washington state, Deloria served as a lecturer at the College of Ethnic Studies at Western Washington State College, in Bellingham. He also was a delegate to the White House Conference on Youth and a consultant to Educational Challenges, Inc., in Washington, D.C.

Deloria continued to write books. *Of Utmost Good Faith*, published in 1971, is a technical documentation of significant treaties, acts, and rulings that affect Indians. He also edited and revised *Red Man in the New World Drama* in 1972, an account of North American Indian history written during the 1930's.

In 1971, Deloria founded the Institute for the Development of Indian Law in Washington, D.C. He played a behind-the-scenes role in the return of Blue Lake to the Taos Pueblo and was a White House guest at the bill's signing. He also continued to help Indian tribes receive formal recognition and assistance from the government and was instrumental in getting the state of New York to return original Six Nations wampum belts, which had been confiscated by the state museum in 1909. (Wampum belts are long beaded belts with sacred symbols that mark special events. The belts are necessary for performing some traditional ceremonies.)

During the early 1970s, Deloria also served on the board of directors for the Model Urban Indian Centers Project in San Francisco and the Oglala Sioux Legal Rights Foundation in Pine Ridge, South Dakota. He served on the editorial boards of several publications including that of the American Indian Historical

Society, the Smithsonian's *Handbook of North American Indians*, the *Historical Magazine of the Episcopal Church*, and *Colorado Magazine*. From 1976 to 1988, Deloria served on the Indian committee of the American Civil Liberties Union, was a consultant to the American Lutheran Church, and on the advisory council of the Nebraska Educational Television Network, and he served on such boards as the Denver Public Library Foundation, Museum of the American Indian, and the Indian Rights Association. In 1974, Deloria published two books on Indian law: *Behind the Trail of Broken Treaties* and *The Indian Affair*. In 1977, he published an informative book for young adults, *Indians of the Pacific Northwest*.

Deloria was not an AIM leader, nor did he take part in the occupation of BIA headquarters or of Wounded Knee in 1973 because he "saw no point to a lot of the demonstrations." Although the national recognition received by AIM during the early seventies "might have been a morale booster," says Deloria, its leaders "never thought through what they wanted the U.S. to do." When the Wounded Knee trials began, however, it became a different story. Seeing a chance to get some definitive statements on the Sioux treaties, Deloria served as expert witness and attorney in four of the trials. He got the Fort Laramie Treaty of 1868 introduced into court as evidence of the motives of the protestors. He also argued one of the cases on appeal. He was the only Indian attorney involved in these trials.

Besides writing books in history, politics, and law, Deloria wrote about religion. *God Is Red*, a call to a new religious freedom, was published in 1973. (An updated version of the book came out in 1994.) "Only by returning to the land can we have an adequate idea of God," Deloria proclaimed, comparing traditional Indian religions to Christianity and boldly stating that Christianity had failed. As a result of this book of innovative theology intertwined with history and science, in 1974 Deloria was named one of 11 Theological Superstars of the Future and was featured in an article in *Time* magazine. In 1979, Deloria published *The Metaphysics of Modern Existence*, a book that attempts to integrate science and religion. In it, he stated that "the manner in which primitive, tribal people understood the world and the way we must now understand the world are identical."

In 1978, Deloria took a position as a professor at the University of Arizona in Tucson. He was instrumental in starting a master's

Vine Deloria, Jr., 1995.

program in Indian Studies, from which a number of graduates have gone on to work for tribes or teach at universities. He also published two books with coauthor Clifford Lytle, also a professor at the university. *American Indians, American Justice* (1983) is a comprehensive overview of law and politics as concerns the Indian. *The Nations Within: The Past and Future of American Indian Sovereignty* (1984) is a historical account of the development of John Collier's New Deal for Indians in the 1930s, explaining the complexity of American Indian relationships with federal and state government and supporting self-rule for tribes.

In 1990, Deloria accepted a position at the University of Colorado in Boulder, where he teaches history, primarily that of the post–Civil War West. Deloria also teaches a class in law or religious studies every year or so. He continues to lecture at universities nationwide and to speak out for Indians. He was a recent plaintiff, for example, in a legal petition against offensive references to Indians ("redskin," "tomahawk chop") by professional sports teams.

Deloria's ideas remain strong. In a 1990 interview with *The Progressive* magazine, Deloria remarks that he should have been even harsher on the United States in his book, *Custer Died for Your Sins.* "In less than 200 years, Americans have virtually ruined the whole continent," he says, adding that white people are "desperately trying to get some relationship to Earth, but it's all in their heads." His solution for Indians:

> *Take a two-million-acre reservation; run buffalo and cattle, let people live wherever they want, go to school if they want, learn the old ways if they want, perfectly respectable to be a cowboy and not see a day of school, go back to basics (food, shelter, clothing), and tell the rest of the world to [stay away].*

His current passion, however, is the work he is doing through the American Indian Science and Engineering Society (AISES), an organization associated with the University of Colorado. Through the society, Deloria has planned conferences to recover such traditional Indian science as growing food in the desert, knowledge of the stars, and relationships with animals. Presenters at the conferences are traditional elders from tribes across the continent. The conferences are elder-oriented, which means they are open only to Indians and that no note-taking or photos are allowed. Elders compare their tribal knowledge about past events and exchange ideas on their nation's pre-Columbian history.

Several conferences on star knowledge have been held in planetariums that allowed the elder teachers to manipulate a model of the sky while telling their stories. These conferences have exposed much knowledge that no other culture has access to. Sioux traditions, for example, speak of a star in the middle of the Big Dipper, whereas today scientists know that a black hole exists in the middle of the constellation. From this, scientists can conclude that centuries ago the sky had more stars in it than it does today.

Deloria's latest book, *Red Earth, White Lies* (1995), deals with the origin of American Indians. Some scholars believe Indians migrated to North America over the Bering Strait some 15,000 years ago. Their theory also holds Indians responsible for the demise of such giant animals as mammoths, sabertooth tigers, and giant buffalo. Indian mythology, however, states that Indians migrated from other continents by boat or originated on this continent. Indian tradition also does not support the idea of Indians killing off species of animals. Deloria attempts to refute the Bering Strait theory in his book by showing that the extinction of these giant animals was due to a natural catastrophe, such as a flood that may have occurred at the same time as the biblical "deluge" in the Middle East. His book is meant as a rebuttal to persons who use the Bering Strait theory as reasons to deny current tribes hunting and fishing rights.

Indian leaders' biggest challenge, according to Deloria, is to modify the ways intellectuals talk and write about Indians that have caused Indians to be seen as inferior. Change must occur not only on the political front, he believes, but in subject areas across the board at universities nationwide. Whatever avenue he pursues, Deloria has the same goal: improving life for his people through a better understanding of Indian history and culture by the non-Indian majority.

Awards Received by Vine Deloria, Jr.

Anisfield Wolf Award, for *Custer Died for Your Sins*, 1970
Special Citation for *We Talk, You Listen*, National Conference
   of Christians and Jews, 1971
Indian Achievement Award, Indian Council Fire, 1972
Theological Superstar of the Future, *Interchurch Features*, 1974

Honorary Degrees; University Honors
Honorary Doctor of Humane Letters, Augustana Lutheran
   Seminary, Rock Island, Illinois, 1972
Honorary Doctor of Letters, Scholastica College, Duluth,
   Minnesota, 1976
Distinguished Alumni Award, Iowa State University, Ames,
   Iowa, 1977
Honorary Professor, Athabasca University, Edmonton, Cali-
   fornia, 1977
Honorary Doctor of Humane Letters, Hamline University, St.
   Paul, Minnesota, 1979
Distinguished Alumni in the Field of Legal Education,
   University of Colorado School of Law, Boulder, Colo-
   rado, 1985

AMERICAN INDIAN MOVEMENT (AIM) LEADERS

Dissenters and Activists

This is the last chance for the American Indian people to get our treaty rights, not only before the public of the United States and the public of the world, but into your courts . . . We want recognition as a people, by the White House. . . .

. . . I'm not going to die in some barroom brawl. I'm not going to die in a car wreck on some lonely road on the reservation because I've been drinking to escape the oppression of this society. I'm not going to die when I walk into Pine Ridge and Dickie's goons feel I should be offed. That's not the way I'm going to die. I'm going to die fighting for my treaty rights. Period.

> —Russell Means, national AIM leader
> in negotiations with federal officials
> at Wounded Knee II

A caravan of cars filled with American Indian Movement (AIM) activists left Calico Hall on the Pine Ridge Indian Reservation in South Dakota on February 27, 1973. (Pine Ridge is the home of the Oglala Lakota, sometimes referred to as Sioux.) Although they were thought to be traveling to Porcupine, a town with a larger meeting hall, the group instead stopped at the small village of Wounded Knee, consisting mostly of a Catholic church and a trading post. The militant group took over the village, holding its 11 residents hostage, and later officially declared it to be an Independent Oglala Nation.

Federal Bureau of Investigation (FBI) agents, Bureau of Indian Affairs (BIA) agents, and U.S. marshals were already in the area to protect the BIA building at Pine Ridge. Considering the siege an act of treason, they quickly surrounded Wounded Knee and blocked off the four roads. A short while later, militant supporters of tribal president Richard Wilson, who opposed AIM and were called goons or "the Goon Squad", moved in and claimed jurisdiction over the situation. They established their own roadblocks in front of the FBI and marshals' roadblocks. Gunfire was exchanged almost nightly.

The incident brought instant international news coverage, and negotiations between federal officials and AIM leaders began almost immediately. On March 10, federal officials lifted the roadblocks, hoping that the people would disperse; instead, the number of people doubled from about 200 to 400, including Indians from other tribes and a few non-Indians. The Oglala Lakota traditional chiefs and holy men from Pine Ridge also went to Wounded Knee to support the dissenters. Other Oglala felt it was safer to be at Wounded Knee than on reservation because of the actions of Richard Wilson.

Although the stand-off ended after 71 days, it only worsened the situation between Richard Wilson's supporters and AIM, which was backed by the traditional people. Wilson had flatly stated, "AIM will die at Wounded Knee" and "I will not be responsible for holding my people back. If necessary, I will join them with my guns." During the next three years, more than 60 AIM members died violently on the Pine Ridge Reservation, including leaders Pedro Bissonnette and Anna Mae Aquash.

AIM nevertheless survived through the continued work of such leaders as Clyde Bellecourt, Dennis Banks, and Russell Means. Although not as active and no longer a militant group, its chapters work independently to promote Indian self-determination and the recognition of treaty rights. They also sponsor charitable and educational services for Indians.

Dennis Banks

Anishinabe
AIM National Leader
(1937–   )

Dennis Banks was born in 1937 on the Leech Lake Indian Reservation in northern Minnesota. He is Anishinabe, an Indian nation sometimes referred to as Chippewa or Ojibwa. Sent to BIA boarding school from age five through high school, Banks lost his ability to speak his native language.

He joined the U.S. Air Force in 1953 and served for three years in Japan. When he returned, Banks was unable to find a job and spent the next 10 years as a drifter, drinking heavily. In 1966, he was sentenced to two years in prison for burglary.

In Minneapolis in 1968, Banks met with George Mitchell and Clyde Bellecourt (also Anishinabe) regarding the social conditions of native people in Minneapolis, Minnesota. Because the men saw prejudice as a source of many of the Indians' problems and wanted to do something about it, they founded the American Indian Movement (AIM). As Banks recalled later:

> [We] were tired of begging for welfare, tired of being scapegoats in America and decided to start building on the strengths of our own people; decided to build our own schools; our own job training problems; and our own destiny. That was our motivation to begin.

Their first priority was to reduce police brutality, which they accomplished by taking pictures of arrests of Indians and informing arrestees of their rights. According to Banks, they were them-

selves often beaten by police and thrown into jail for their inter-
ference. The group also worked to improve housing conditions
and employment for Indians in Minneapolis. A sincere and
thoughtful leader, Banks was elected chairman of AIM in 1969.

As AIM membership increased, Banks and Bellecourt were able
to establish a court advocacy program in which mothers reported
on racism within the Minneapolis juvenile court system, and
secure *pro bono* lawyers for Indians through the Legal Justice
Center. The two men also worked with the public school system
to rid the schools of racist textbooks. Eventually, AIM founded its
own schools, where students learn their native languages, culture,
and history from an Indian perspective.

As word of AIM's successes spread, other AIM chapters sprang
up in 43 states across the U.S. Banks visited AIM chapters and spoke
on behalf of AIM at national Indian conventions. Then AIM began
to stage demonstrations nationwide to get the media's attention.

In 1970, Banks and Bellecourt organized a confrontation with
the National Council of Churches (NCC). The two men and sup-

*Dennis Banks (center) spoke for the recognition of Fort Laramie treaty rights
at an AIM protest on July 4, 1975, at the Washington Monument in the
Black Hills. He is flanked by Floyd "Red Crow" Westerman (left), Clyde
Bellecourt (behind Banks), and Bill Means (right).* (© Kevin McKiernan)

porters interrupted an NCC convention in Detroit, challenging church leaders to work more effectively with Indians. As a result, many churches established direct communication with Indian leaders who were able to get church funds to the communities that most needed help. Many churches also began to provide funds for AIM activities.

Banks and Bellecourt traveled also that year to Sault Ste. Marie, Michigan, where they successfully persuaded other Anishinabe to end their participation in a pageant that honored the Jesuits who brought "godliness to the heathens." Also in 1970, Banks and Bellecourt interrupted a Thanksgiving celebration in Plymouth, Massachusetts, and even took over a replica of Christopher Columbus's ship, the *Mayflower II*. And they claimed Indian land by camping at Mount Rushmore in the Black Hills of South Dakota in 1970, 1971, and again in 1975.

Many people were uncomfortable with AIM's use of tough talk, threats, guns, and violence, These people said that AIM spoke for only a small portion of American Indians. Yet their activities did awaken pride among Indians, and they received the support of traditional elders and holy men.

Banks and other AIM leaders were willing to support any Indian who asked for their help. When Raymond Yellow Thunder, an Oglala Lakota from Gordon, Nebraska, was murdered by four white men, Banks and others went to South Dakota at his family's request to demand justice. During that time, Banks also traveled through Nebraska and South Dakota, collecting complaints about other incidents of brutality and racism against Indians. Although Banks turned the affidavits over to the government, no action was ever taken.

In 1972, AIM organized a caravan that traveled from the West Coast across the United States to Washington, D.C. Banks flew out to California and led the contingent that started from San Francisco. Along the way, the caravan stopped at reservations and Indian schools, attracting supporters. Called the Trail of Broken Treaties, Banks and other AIM leaders wanted to draw attention to the many treaties the U.S. government had broken with the Indian nations.

Banks was dissatisfied with the reception from the national BIA headquarters in Washington, D.C. On November 2, 1972, as they were leaving the BIA building, a scuffle broke out between some of the younger Indians and building guards. AIM seized the building. Dennis Banks was quoted in *U.S. News & World Report* as saying:

> *We're trying to bring about some meaningful change for the Indian community. If this is the only action [takeover of BIA headquarters in Washington, D.C.] that will bring change, then you can count on demonstrations like this 365 days a year.*

During the eight-day occupation of the BIA building, Banks arranged for files that contained evidence of BIA's illegal activities to be taken. Much of the content of the files was later published in a newspaper column. AIM members finally left the building when they were allowed to present a Twenty Points solution paper to President Richard Nixon, and the White House gave them a $66,000 grant to cover travel expenses home.

Banks and most of the other demonstrators went to the Pine Ridge Reservation for a victory celebration. Tension on the reservation between AIM and the tribal government was high. Tribal Chair Richard Wilson had received federal funds to hire more police, and these officers, according to AIM, harassed any opponents. Banks was arrested for violating a tribal court restraining order against his presence and removed from the reservation. Wilson, because he controlled reservation jobs and money, was believed to have bought the loyalty of his supporters. In addition, many traditional people felt that Wilson was merely a puppet for the federal government. Although four attempts had been made to impeach Wilson, they had all been unsuccessful.

Then Wesley Bad Heart Bull was killed in a bar in Buffalo Gap, South Dakota. When police hesitated to arrest his killer, Banks and other protestors went to the county seat in Custer where they occupied and eventually burned down the courthouse. The occu-

Excerpts from the Fort Laramie Treaty of 1868

Article I.
From this day forward all war between the parties to this agreement shall forever cease. . . .

Article II.
The United States agrees that . . . the east bank of the Missouri River where the forty-sixth parallel of north latitude crosses the same, thence along low-water mark down said east bank to a point opposite where the northern line of the State of Nebraska strikes the river, thence west across said river, and along the northern line of Nebraska to the one hundred and fourth degree of longitude west from Greenwich, thence north on said meridian to a point where the forty-sixth parallel of north latitude intercepts the same, then due east along said parallel to the place of the beginning . . . is set apart for the absolute and undisturbed use and occupation of the Indians herein named . . . and the United States now solemnly agrees that no persons except those herein designated and authorized so to do . . . shall ever be permitted to pass over, settle upon, or reside in the territory described in this article . . .

Article XII.
No treaty for the cession of any portion or part of the reservation herein described . . . shall be of any validity or force as against the said Indians, unless executed and signed by at least three fourths of all adult male Indians, occupying or interested in the same . . .

Article XVI.
The United States hereby agrees and stipulates that the country north of the North Platte river and east of the summits of the Big Horn mountains shall be held and considered to be unceded Indian territory, and also stipulates and agrees that no white person or persons shall be permitted to settle upon or occupy any portion of the same, or without the consent of the Indians . . . And it is further agreed by the United States that within ninety days after the conclusion of peace with all bands of the Sioux nation, the military posts now established in the territory of Montana shall be closed.

pation of Wounded Knee, led by AIM leaders Dennis Banks and Russell Means, followed.

Banks and Means defended the takeover of Wounded Knee on the basis of the 1868 Fort Laramie Treaty, which set apart a large amount of land in the western half of South Dakota, the northwestern part of Nebraska, and small parts of eastern Wyoming and Montana as unceded Indian territory. Since 1868, however, gold had been discovered in Indian holy land, the sacred Black Hills, and the Sioux nations had gradually lost much of this land.

The militants chose Wounded Knee because it was the site of a massacre of unarmed Sioux Ghost Dancers by the U.S. military in 1890. Of the 200 Sioux camped at Wounded Knee, 150 were killed and 50 others injured. The dead were buried at the site in a mass grave and the Sioux never forgot or forgave the United States for this incident.

After declaring Wounded Knee an Independent Oglala Nation on March 11, 1973, AIM leaders sent their demands to the federal government. They wanted Richard Wilson to be removed as tribal chair of Pine Ridge; they wanted the U.S. Senate to investigate the nearly 400 treaties that had been broken; and they also wanted an investigation of the mistreatment of Indians by the BIA.

One of Banks's first actions at Wounded Knee was to call in the press. The stand-off soon became a nightly national TV event, which offered some degree of protection to the outnumbered AIM warriors. To give the illusion of a larger group of warriors, Banks staged "platoon drills" within sight of the surrounding federal forces.

It was Banks who met with federal officials at a roadblock to receive their counterproposal. After reading the proposal in an AIM meeting, however, Banks burned it, stating, "This is what we think of their offer."

The stand-off finally ended on May 8, after federal officials promised that presidential representatives would come to the reservation and discuss violations of the Ft. Laramie Treaty with the traditional chiefs. Although these talks were held, the officials sent had no power and, according to Banks, nothing changed on the reservation.

Dennis Banks served 18 months in the state penitentiary in Sioux Falls, South Dakota, for his conviction on crimes committed at the Custer court-house riot in 1972. (© Kevin McKiernan)

Banks did not sign the accord with the federal government. Nor did he surrender as the others did on May 8, but instead left undercover the night of May 7 and went into hiding in the North-west Territories, Canada, to avoid arrest. Canadian police finally forced the AIM contingent to leave by cutting off all supplies to their remote village. When Banks flew back to the U.S., money had been raised for his bail.

Dennis Banks and Russell Means were tried together in 1974 in St. Paul, Minnesota, for crimes at Wounded Knee. As leaders of the occupation, they were considered responsible for all crimes, whether they took part in them or not. Half of the charges were dismissed for lack of evidence. In July, the government rested its case against them for charges of conspiracy, theft, and assaulting federal officers.

With the help of an excellent team of lawyers, Banks and Means served as their own co-counsel. They also countersued the federal government for BIA misuse of funds, illegal wiretapping at

Wounded Knee, obliterating evidence, allowing FBI agents to perjure themselves, and permitting Richard Wilson to conduct a reign of terror at Pine Ridge.

During breaks in the eight-month trial, Banks continued to do his work as AIM director. He established an AIM office in St. Paul, flew to California to oversee the distribution of food to poor people, and served as the chief negotiator between Wisconsin officials and armed Menominee Indians who had seized an abandoned monastery.

The case went to jury on September 12. When one of the jurors suffered a heart attack, however, the prosecution refused to let the 11-member jury come to a verdict. Judge Alfred Nichol reacted by dismissing the charges. In his statement, he attacked U.S. attorney R. D. Hurd, citing illegal intervention of armed forces, and stated that the FBI had committed numerous illegal acts.

After the Wounded Knee trial, Banks flew to Kenora, Ontario, Canada, where he mediated between local authorities and Indian occupiers of Anishinabe Park. Then he and his Oglala wife, Kamook, and their daughter moved to a tiny cabin three miles east of Oglala on the Pine Ridge Reservation. Soon after, he went on trial for riot charges stemming from the Custer courthouse incident.

When convicted on the Custer charges in August 1975, Banks, fearing for his life in state custody, again went underground, this time to California. In 1976, he was arrested and arraigned in San Francisco for his alleged involvement in an Oregon shoot-out. Police had stopped a trailer home and Banks's wife, Kamook, Anna Mae Aquash, and three other AIM leaders disembarked. Then someone gunned the trailer home's engine and drove away. Law officials believed that man was Banks; charges, however, were eventually dismissed.

Governor Jerry Brown of California subsequently refused to return Banks to South Dakota, believing his life was in danger. Banks was free as long as he stayed in California. He earned an associate of arts degree from Davis University and served as chancellor at Deganawida Quetzecoatl University (an all Indian-controlled school).

In 1978, Banks organized "The Longest Walk." He sent several hundred AIM marchers from San Francisco to Washington, D.C., for a mass rally at the Washington Monument, where they delivered a manifesto challenging the definition of self-determination and demanding acknowledgment of tribes' rights to sovereignty. Eventually the issue was brought to the United Nations.

When Governor Jerry Brown left office in 1983, Banks sought refuge on the Onondaga Reservation in upstate New York. While there, he organized the Jim Thorpe Longest Run (from New York to Los Angeles) for the Jim Thorpe Memorial Games. Thorpe, a Sac and Fox-Potawatomi Indian from Oklahoma, won two track and field gold medals at the 1912 Olympic Games. The medals, however, were taken from him afterward since he was not considered an amateur athlete because he once accepted money for playing baseball. Banks was later able to arrange for Thorpe's Olympic gold medals to be returned to the Thorpe family at the Jim Thorpe Memorial Games in Los Angeles.

Dennis Banks at the Sacred Run event in New Zealand, 1993.
(© Alice Lambert)

Tired of hiding, Banks surrendered in 1985 to law officials in South Dakota and served 18 months in prison. After his release, Banks worked as a drug and alcohol counselor at a school on the Pine Ridge Reservation. He also was instrumental in persuading Honeywell to open a computer assembly facility in Oglala, on the Pine Ridge Reservation, increasing jobs.

In addition to his involvement with native American issues and AIM events, Dennis Banks directs the Sacred Run Foundation, an international multicultural organization that sponsors running and cultural events. The organization is dedicated to spreading the message of the sacredness of all things and the need to maintain balance between humans and Earth. The group organizes runs each year and, by 1996, had clocked over 56,000 miles.

Russell Means

Oglala Lakota/Yankton Dakota
AIM National Leader
(1940–   )

Russell Means was born in 1940 to a Yankton Dakota mother and an Oglala Lakota father near Greenwood, South Dakota. (Both Dakota and Lakota are sometimes referred to as Sioux.) The family moved to the Oakland area of California when Russell was only three years old. His father, an excellent welder, worked at the shipyards when he was not away on drinking binges. Russell describes his mother as a caring but nervous woman who often beat her boys. Each summer they returned to South Dakota, where Russell attended pow-wows and learned about Indian ways.

Although the Means family lived in a racially mixed neighborhood, they were the only Indian family. Russell was an excellent student. His teachers even recommended that he skip a grade or two, but his mother wanted him to remain in a class with children his own age.

Before he started high school, Russell's family bought a house and moved to San Leandro, a predominantly white community. Bored and small for his age, Russell felt that he didn't fit in. He stopped taking his studies seriously and instead skipped school, stole, and drank alcohol with Chicano friends. Worried, his mother sent him to live for a year with relatives on the Winnebago Reservation in Nebraska. When he returned, Russell began selling marijuana and other drugs to high school students. It was only with encouragement from a couple of favorite teachers that Russell graduated from San Leandro High School in 1958.

For the next 10 years, Russell drifted in and out of several jobs, schools, and states. He gave up drugs, but continued to drink heavily and get into barroom brawls. He attended Sawyer Business School in Los Angeles, got married, took a job as a ballroom dance instructor in San Francisco, then moved to the Pine Ridge Reservation in South Dakota and took a job in construction. (Pine Ridge is the home of his father's relatives, the Oglala Lakota.) Later, he made money performing traditional Indian dances in Arizona and riding steers at rodeos.

Wanting to continue his education, Russell moved in 1965 to Ottumwa, Iowa, where he studied accounting at Iowa Technical College. He finished his studies in 1966 at Arizona State University in Tempe, Arizona. Finally, Russell moved to Cleveland, where he hoped to avoid his drinking problems and support his wife and children. It was there that he met Clyde Bellecourt and Dennis Banks and became involved in the American Indian Movement.

Means's first AIM event was the confrontation with the National Council of Churches in Detroit. Means also helped to persuade Indians in Sault Ste. Marie, Michigan, to discontinue their performances in the Jesuit pageant, and he participated in the takeover of the *Mayflower II* in Plymouth, Massachusetts, on Thanksgiving Day 1970. He also started and directed the Cleveland chapter of AIM.

Means was an angry but excellent speaker for AIM, and his remarks were quoted in nationwide magazines and newspapers.

*AIM leaders (left to right) Sid Mills, Clyde Bellecourt, and Russell Means
negotiate with U.S. government officials Kent Frizell and Richard Held at
Wounded Knee.* (© Kevin McKiernan)

In 1972, after the beating death of Raymond Yellow Thunder in
South Dakota, for example, Means jokingly called for a march on
Washington to demand a federal law that would make it a crime
to kill an Indian—if all else failed, as an amendment to the Endan-
gered Species Act.

Means led the contingent from Seattle to Washington, D.C.,
during the Trail of Broken Treaties in 1972. After the takeover of
the BIA building, Means supported burning down the building
unless their demands were met. When the White House promised
to consider the Twenty Points, however, he left with the rest of the
contingent for Pine Ridge Reservation.

After several incidents with police at Pine Ridge, Means joined
other AIM members in Custer, South Dakota, to insist that murder
charges be filed against the murderer of Wesley Bad Heart Bull.
Instead, a fight between AIM members and police broke out at the
courthouse, and Means was jailed for riot charges, then released
on bail. Shortly afterward, U.S. marshals surrounded the BIA
office on the Pine Ridge Reservation to protect it from AIM.

In February 1973, Means was present at a meeting between AIM
leaders and the Oglala Lakota traditional chiefs in Calico, South

Dakota. According to Russell Means's autobiography, *Where White Men Fear to Tread*, chief and holy man Frank Fools Crow finally directed AIM to Wounded Knee. "There, you will be protected," he said.

Because of his dedication and willingness to die for his cause, Russell Means served as a strong negotiator for AIM with federal agents during the occupation of Wounded Knee. Meeting with government officials in a tipi in the "demilitarized zone," Means made angry statements that were later quoted in the media, such as: "They [U.S. marshals] brought in the law enforcement agencies to protect buildings rather than protect people's rights out here. And the end result—Wounded Knee."

Regarding recognition of the 1868 Fort Laramie Treaty, Means stated:

> *For two weeks we've known that the United States Government can come in and squash us, militarily. We never thought that we could beat them, overthrow them. But here's the fact: if they come in or not, whether we're massacred or not, they are still going to have to answer to our treaty rights, not only to the Indian people of America, but to all the countries of the world.*

Later, Oglala Lakota holy man Leonard Crow Dog organized a Ghost Dance at Wounded Knee in which participants asked the spirits of their ancestors to protect them. After the dance, Means spoke, comparing the AIM dancers to the religious Ghost Dancers of the 1890s who believed that by dancing the Ghost Dance and remaining true to the ways of their ancestors, they could bring back the "old ways":

> *The white man says that the 1899 massacre [of Ghost Dancers at Wounded Knee] was the end of the wars with the Indian, that it was the end of the Indian, the end of the Ghost Dance. Yet here we are at war, we're still Indians, and we're Ghost Dancing again. And the spirits of Big Foot and his people are all around us. . . .*

On April 5, 1973, AIM leaders signed an agreement with federal agents that allowed Russell Means to go to Washington, D.C., as a negotiator. After leaving Wounded Knee, Means was arrested, jailed, and then released on bond to travel to Washington, D.C.

When he arrived, however, the government refused to negotiate until AIM laid down all weapons at Wounded Knee.

Because he could not return to Wounded Knee, Means went to Los Angeles to raise money for AIM. While there, he was arrested on riot charges for incidents that occurred before Wounded Knee, and spent 43 days in jail. By October 1973, he was on trial in St. Paul for crimes at Wounded Knee. During the trial, Means ran against Richard Wilson for tribal chair of Pine Ridge. When Wilson won the election, Means and Banks challenged the results, accusing Wilson of stuffing ballot boxes.

In St. Paul, Means and Banks served as their own co-counsel, objecting often and dragging the trial out for eight months. At one point, the defense attorneys with whom Means and Banks consulted were thrown out of the courtroom and jailed for contempt. Then a fist fight broke out between U.S. marshals and AIM supporters watching the trial.

Means was shocked, he claims in his autobiography, at the many lies told by government witnesses as well as the illegal actions they admitted to. When an FBI agent testified he had violated electronic surveillance law, Means and Banks tried to place him under citizen's arrest. Judge Alfred Nichol apparently was horrified at the illegalities of the prosecution as well. When the jury was not able to come to a decision because one juror was ill, Nichol dismissed all charges against Means and Banks. Both men still had other cases pending against them, however.

Russell Means returned to Pine Ridge to continue his work, even though threats had been made against his life by supporters of Richard Wilson. In confrontations with tribal police, Means was shot in the back and the chest, a bullet grazed his forehead, and his eye was gouged by a rifle. He recovered from all injuries.

Means was tried for violent crimes seven times without a conviction. Then he was sentenced and served thirty days in jail for his part in the Custer courthouse riot. Later, he received a four-year sentence on an earlier conflict with police at a Sioux Falls courthouse, and served a year during 1978–79 in the state penitentiary in Sioux Falls, South Dakota. There, Means received a warm welcome from other Indian inmates who saw him as a hero, but was stabbed in the chest by a non-Indian inmate. Means recovered and used his time to write letters on AIM's behalf and study law in the prison's library.

In 1981, Means led a group of AIM members to establish Yellow Thunder Camp in the Black Hills, announcing it as the first step in the reoccupation of their holy land. The U.S. Forest Service filed suit for eviction, but AIM members, including Russell Means, lived at the camp for several years. Finally, the U.S. government awarded them $2 million for the land, but no Sioux have been willing to accept the check, stating instead they want the Black Hills back.

Russell Means (in white hat and jacket) confronts a tribal police officer at the Pine Ridge Hospital during an AIM march to improve health care in 1985. (© Kevin McKiernan)

In 1983, Means made another bid for the tribal presidency at Pine Ridge. His platform included reinstating the traditional Oglala elders' councils as the primary government and severing all ties with the federal government. Opponents successfully had Means barred from the ballot, however, because of his conviction and prison term.

In 1984, Means traveled among the Miskito Indians in Nicaragua, who he claims were being mistreated by the Sandinistas—rebels whom AIM had earlier supported. His decision caused a rift between himself and other AIM leaders. The following year, Means arranged a speaking tour with the Unification Church, during which time he spoke about what was happening to the Miskito Indians. He also returned to the Pine Ridge Reservation where he took part in a confrontation with tribal police at Pine Ridge Hospital during a march to improve health care.

Means ran unsuccessfully in 1986 for nomination as the presidential candidate of the Libertarian Party. Then, living in New Mexico, he attempted several business liaisons between Indian tribes and foreign nations that failed.

In 1991, Means was asked to play the role of Chingachgook in the movie, *The Last of the Mohicans*. This began a new career as an actor, which Means believes gives him media opportunities to speak out for Indian rights. He has since acted in several films and lent his voice to Chief Powhatan in Disney's *Pocahontas*.

Even 20 years after Wounded Knee, Means realized he was still an angry man. Knowing how little it took to make him angry, Means finally admitted he had a serious problem with anger and entered treatment in Tucson, Arizona, in December 1991. He discovered that much of his anger was a response he had learned in childhood and had never outgrown. He also learned that many other people, not only Indians, had good reasons to be angry.

After therapy, Means announced he had adopted a policy of nonviolence and has talked of plans to build a treatment center for therapy based on traditional Indian values at Pine Ridge and to rebuild the Oglala Lakota nation. He ends his autobiography with this statement: "With honesty and with therapy, my people can be made whole again."

Anna Mae Pictou Aquash

Micmac
AIM National Leader
(1945–1976)

Anna Mae Pictou was born in 1945 on the Micmac reservation near Shubenacadie, Nova Scotia, Canada. She lived with her mother, Mary Ellen Pictou, and two older sisters in a dilapidated house along a dirt road. Her father, Francis Thomas Levi, had left to work in a logging camp in Maine. When her mother married Noel Sapier in 1949, Anna Mae and her family moved to Pictou Landing, another reservation in Nova Scotia, where they had no running water, electricity, or central heat. Anna Mae and a sister suffered from tuberculosis that went untreated due to a lack of health care.

Anna Mae was a small but strong, daring, and determined child. She attended a Catholic church every Sunday as well as a Catholic mission school. From age 11 to 14, Anna Mae attended school in New Glasgow, but when her stepfather died of cancer, the family moved back to the Shubenacadie reserve. When Anna Mae was 16 years old, her mother suddenly married again and left her children behind. The next summer, Anna Mae joined friends to pick potatoes in Maine. She met Micmac Jake Maloney and moved to Boston with him in search of work and a better future. After giving birth to two daughters, Denise and Deborah, Anna Mae married Jake and began working in a sewing factory.

Intelligent and eager to learn, Anna Mae taught herself to type and play the guitar. She liked to read child psychology. She lived in a nice apartment and wore a bleached beehive hairdo. After her husband left her for a white woman, however, Anna Mae began drinking and even got into several fights. Through a group therapy program for Indian alcoholics, Anna Mae became involved with the Boston Indian Council (BIC), where she joined a successful picket line against its non-Indian executive director, then became a volunteer community worker. She was present with

Anna Mae Pictou married Nogeeshik Aquash on April 12, 1973, in a traditional Lakota ceremony during the siege at Wounded Knee. Although the marriage did not last, Anna Mae kept her husband's last name.
(© Kevin McKiernan)

other BIC members at the 1970 AIM demonstration at the *Mayflower II* on Thanksgiving Day, 1970.

That same year, Anna Mae began teaching at TRIBE, an Indian learning and cultural center in Maine. She taught academic subjects as well as art, crafts, music, and dancing. She also reviewed textbooks for their treatment of Indians, explored ways to instill pride and motivation in Indian youth, and became known as someone who was in a hurry to effect change.

When the project was terminated, Anna Mae enrolled in a New Careers program at Boston's Wheelock College, where she attended classes and worked as a teaching assistant at a day-care center. Anna Mae was exceptionally good with children, even baking and writing songs for them. When offered a scholarship to Brandeis University, Anna Mae turned it down, preferring to continue her community work. She and other BIC members joined AIM protestors in the occupation of the BIA building in Washington, D.C., in 1972. When the occupation of Wounded Knee took place, she and her boyfriend, Chippewa Nogeeshik Aquash, left her children with Anna Mae's sister and joined the protest for about a month, where they were married.

Anna Mae was a strong worker at Wounded Knee, retaining a sense of humor. She made clandestine trips to bring food into the besieged village, helped dig bunkers, and took part in nightly patrols of the village. She and her husband left Wounded Knee before the occupancy ended, and Anna Mae was charged only with violating reservation law for her participation.

After Wounded Knee, Aquash traveled across the country, taking part in AIM events. In Ottawa, Ontario, Canada, she set up an exhibit of native beadwork and jewelry. In 1974, during the Dennis Banks and Russell Means trial, Aquash lived in St. Paul and worked as a teacher at AIM's Red School House. She also had a short affair with Dennis Banks.

When the trial ended, Aquash went to Los Angeles to help set up a West Coast AIM office. Another staffer, Douglass Durham, was later found to be an FBI informant. According to staffer Dino Butler in *In the Spirit of Crazy Horse*: "Anna Mae just couldn't stand Doug; she was on to him. She was a smart woman. She'd just kick him out of the office: 'Go sleep in your van! You're not coming in here!'"

When the West Coast office flourished because of her fund-raising efforts, Aquash's reputation as a national AIM leader grew. She returned to St. Paul, where she organized a successful benefit concert for the Red School House. Then in 1975, she moved to the Pine Ridge Reservation, along with other AIM leaders, to help defend the Oglala traditional people from the violent Goon Squad. While there, she organized the women in fund-raising events and in demanding improvements in a federal food program.

On June 26, 1975, a shoot-out between FBI agents and AIM members and supporters occurred on the reservation, in which two FBI agents and one Indian were killed. Aquash was on the list of persons the FBI wanted to question when investigating the FBI agents' deaths, even though she had been in Cedar Rapids, Iowa, at the time. Aquash was arrested in an FBI raid in September and charged with possession of a firearm with an obliterated serial number. (Leonard Peltier was later found guilty and sent to prison for the deaths of the two FBI agents.)

While being questioned by FBI Agent David Price, Aquash later told friends, he told her if she didn't cooperate she would not live out the year. Aquash also told her attorney she thought her life was in danger. According to interrogation transcripts, Aquash had refused to talk to Price, saying only: "You can either shoot me or throw me in jail as those are the two choices I am taking. That's what you're going to do with me anyway."

After being released on bail, Aquash continued her fund-raising efforts. She was arrested in November in Oregon along with Kamook Banks and other AIM leaders when their trailer home was stopped by police searching for fugitive Dennis Banks. Oregon authorities returned Aquash to South Dakota to face the weapons charge. Aquash had written to her sister:

> *South Dakota is a very racist state, I am sure I will be sent up even though it is my first arrest. . . . I knew that it would come. . . . My efforts to raise the consciousness of whites who are so against Indians in the States are bound to be stopped by the FBI sooner or later.*

Although she was to go on trial the next day, a judge in South Dakota surprisingly released Aquash into the custody of her attorney. That night Aquash slipped out of a motel room and fled. Because of her good luck in avoiding prison, some AIM leaders began to wonder whether she might be an FBI informant, and even questioned her about it. Despite their lack of confidence, Aquash continued to work for AIM.

On February 24, 1976, a rancher near Wanblee, South Dakota, discovered the body of a woman in a ditch and called authorities. FBI agents cut off the unidentified woman's hands and sent them to FBI headquarters in Washington, D.C., for identification. An autopsy concluded that the woman had died of exposure, and she was buried in a Catholic cemetery at Pine Ridge. The next day, the FBI confirmed the body was that of Anna Mae Aquash.

AIM leaders, outraged at the way the body had been treated, demanded a second autopsy, which showed Aquash had been executed by a gunshot at close range to the back of her head. She was reburied in Oglala, South Dakota, in a traditional Lakota ceremony on March 12. Dennis Banks, fighting extradition to South Dakota from a San Francisco jail, declared the day of her funeral a national Indian day of mourning.

Although more than 20 years have passed since Aquash's murder, it has never been solved. Many people allege it was the work of the Goon Squad, whose members had gone to "clean out" a town near where her body was found, although the disgraceful treatment the FBI afforded the case after her body was found leads some to suspect them. Other suspects include AIM members who believed she was an informant. A fresh investigation was begun in 1995 by U.S. Marshal Robert Ecoffey, a Sioux who once worked for the BIA.

CARRIE DANN

Western Shoshone
Land Rights Activist

(1934–)

I'm saying that my land has never been for sale. This land is my mother. I cannot and will not sell her. My first law is to follow the Creator, and I will not break that. But I will break the laws of man if I have to.
—Carrie Dann
(*The Book of Elders*, 1994)

Agents of the Bureau of Land Management (BLM) claimed the land belonged to the federal government. But Carrie Dann and her sister Mary claimed the land in Crescent Valley, Nevada, was Western Shoshone land. In the fall of 1992, the BLM rounded up about 200 horses in the disputed land under the Wild Horse and Burro Act. Expecting protests from the Dann family, they brought along deputies from the Eureka County Sheriff Department to blockade the roads.

Carrie and her family had been protesting their right to the land for nearly 20 years, but she had never seen her brother Clifford so upset. When she arrived, Clifford doused himself with gasoline and threatened to blow himself up if the sheriff didn't give him access to the Dann livestock.

As Carrie watched, law enforcers knocked her brother to the ground. When Carrie tried to intervene, she was held by the collar and choked. Clifford was arrested and taken to jail.

With her brother facing charges, Carrie had two problems to deal with—her brother's upcoming trial and the continued dispute over land rights. Physically strong from working on the ranch, Carrie had become strong in emotional and spiritual ways, too, as she fought for her tribe's land.

Carrie was born in a traditional Western Shoshone birthing hut in 1934. Her family's land lies between the Shoshone Range and the Cortez Mountains in north central Nevada. The Western Shoshone survived on this desert land for centuries by digging roots and hunting rabbits and other wild game. In the fall they harvested pine nuts, grinding them into a flour that, along with dried meats, sustained them through the snowy winter months.

Carrie's father, Dewey Dann, was originally a farmer from Grass Gully. Whenever he and his brothers planted their fields, however, white neighbors drove cattle onto the fields or set the fields on fire to destroy the crops. Finally, the brothers gave up trying to farm that land.

When Carrie's father married her mother, he moved to his wife's home in Crescent Valley, in accordance with traditional Indian ways. He could see that the land had water coming from the mountains and was good land. Although he heard rumors that he was not welcome, he was determined to become a rancher. Finally, he was able to purchase six hundred and forty acres of land.

Carrie's mother had grown up in Crescent Valley like her mother and grandmother before her. She followed many of the traditional Western Shoshone ways by gathering and drying local wild foods. She also prepared deer meat for her family and kept a large garden. Carrie's sister Mary was born in 1924, followed by several other children. Then Clifford was born in 1932, and Carrie in 1934. The family was a close-knit and hard-working family, but poor. The children spoke only the Shoshone language until they went to school.

Carrie attended public school instead of the Indian boarding school run by the Bureau of Indian Affairs (BIA) as her older brother had done. Her parents believed she would get a better education in the public schools. Carrie also could live at home and take part in the family's traditional ceremonies.

The family was especially busy with ceremonies—private family gatherings to give blessings and thanks—in the fall and spring of each year. Carrie's maternal grandmother taught the children these rituals. Carrie remembers picking pine nuts in preparation for the ceremonies.

Carrie's grandmother often talked to her grandchildren about problems they would face in the future. Her grandmother predicted that they would have further land disputes with the U.S. government, saying that lawyers would lie to them. Carrie now says her grandmother was right.

Carrie married and had children, but eventually moved with her children back to the family ranch, where her brother Clifford worked. Her sister Mary did not marry and continued to live and work at the ranch.

In the spring of 1973, when Carrie was 39 years old, Mary was stopped by a BLM agent as she was herding cattle on land outside their ranch, land used for grazing by other ranchers in the valley. The agent asked to see a herding permit. Their father had purchased and renewed his permit, but the sisters stopped payments, believing the land was Western Shoshone land. The agent, however, said the land was public land. He claimed the Danns' cattle were overgrazing, or eating too much grass, which would result in land erosion. The BLM charged the Danns with trespassing.

That summer Carrie sent several letters to the BLM, asking them to show proof of government ownership of the land. The Western Shoshone Nation had signed a peace treaty called the Treaty of Ruby Valley with the United States in 1863, one year before Nevada became a state. The treaty granted settlers the right to pass through Western Shoshone territory, but did not cede title of the land, about 55 million acres, to the United States.

In 1974, the BLM brought a lawsuit against the Danns. The lawsuit was eventually heard by the U.S. Supreme Court, which declared that, according to the Indian Claims Commission, Western Shoshone title to the land ended in 1872 due to "gradual encroachment," or settlement on the land by non-Indians. In other words, the Indians had lost their land without ever having freely relinquished it, even though this action was prohibited by the Northwest Ordinance signed by the U.S. founding fathers in 1787, which states that the Indians' "lands and liberty shall never be taken from them without their consent; and in their property, rights, and liberty, they shall never be invaded or disturbed . . ."

In 1979, the U.S. Supreme Court awarded the Western Shoshone Nation $26 million for land that had been taken from them. The amount was based on the price of land in 1872, or one dollar an acre; today the land is worth two hundred dollars an acre. Cecil Andrus, then U.S. secretary of the interior, accepted the award money on behalf of the tribe, but the Western Shoshone people refused it, and Dann, with the support of her nation, has continued to fight.

Meanwhile, the Danns filed a countersuit against the BLM, charging that the land belonged to the Western Shoshone Nation, not the U.S. government. Two months after the money was awarded, a district court in Nevada ruled against the Danns' claim because they had been compensated for the land. In 1985, the Supreme Court upheld this ruling, claiming the disputed land did not belong to the Western Shoshone, even though the Danns had used it for several generations. According to an article in *The State of Native America* edited by M. Annette Jaimes, this decision may allow Indians to be evicted from their family lands even though they receive no money for the land.

During the 1980s, the BLM began to allow the cutting of trees on the disputed land. Several of the trees in Crescent Valley were considered sacred to the Dann family. Called ceremonial trees, they played a role in the family's annual ceremonies. These trees

Mary and Carrie Dann.   (Ronnie Farley from *Women of the Native Struggle*)

were part of the one million acres of piñon pines that have been chopped down. Disillusioned by the way the BLM treated the sacred land, Dann has not had the heart to visit the site again. As she stated in *Women of the Native American Struggle* by Ronnie Farley:

> Indigenous women, they're supposed to look at themselves as the Earth. That is the way we were brought up. This is what I try to tell the young people, especially young girls.
>   In the Western Shoshone way a long time ago, when your mother got old, you didn't throw her away; you brought her into your home and took care of her. This is the way we are supposed to take care of the Earth, too. The same way we would take care of our mothers. It's basically just common sense.

The Dann sisters started the Dann Defense Project in 1991. They changed the name in 1992 to Western Shoshone Defense Project (WSDP) and work with volunteers, both Indian and non-Indian, not only for land rights but other Western Shoshone issues such as local law, mining, fishing, and water rights. The WSDP maintains an office in the town of Crescent Valley and has international support. Their goal is to:

> . . . document and counter all acts of aggression against the rights and traditional lands of the Western Shoshone through peaceful and nonviolent means. . . . the Western Shoshone and many other indigenous peoples have been wrongfully denied their sovereignty and lands and we all have a responsibility to help create a just solution to the situation. . . .

In February 1992, the BLM began seizing livestock from the disputed land. Although the Danns had removed most of their herds, several head of cattle and horses remained. Workers from the Western Shoshone Defense Project noticed a gathering of law officials in the town of Crescent Valley. Carrie and Mary drove their truck to the site where their cattle were grazing. On the way, they met a caravan of BLM officials who said they were going to seize any cattle that were trespassing. Carrie responded in anger:

> I started arguing with the BLM agent, and I was getting mad, and the madder I get, the better things go, I guess. I told them that I wasn't going

*to allow them to take my cows. I was determined that the cows weren't
going to go. And I told April, one of the volunteers, "Well, us women first.
If I get arrested, you jump in. . . ."*

According to Carrie Dann, BLM agents also chased their horses
with helicopters, running them through wire fences. Conse-
quently, four of the Dann horses died.

On November 19, 1992, this same event was repeated, with
agents from the sheriff's department brought along to blockade
the roads. The BLM succeeded this time in rounding up about 250
horses. Carrie's brother Clifford, after dousing himself with gasoline, was arrested for assaulting federal officers because the officers got gasoline on their clothes when arresting him. Clifford
Dann was held in a county jail in Reno, Nevada, until his arraignment on November 24. The horses, about 30 of which belonged to
the Danns, were taken to stockyards in Fallon, Nevada.

Always a close family, it was difficult for Carrie and Mary Dann
when they were not allowed to call or visit Clifford in jail. He was
released from jail on his own recognizance at the arraignment on
November 24.

Carrie Dann, now 53, took responsibility for finding an attorney
to represent Clifford at his trial. Together they decided to argue
that the case, having occurred on Western Shoshone land, was
outside U.S. jurisdiction. Because the attorney she hired lived
outside the state of Nevada, however, the judge declared that he
could not represent Clifford Dann. Carrie then became her
brother's counsel. She cross-examined the lawyer on the witness
stand, asking him questions about jurisdictional issues.

Because Carrie Dann believed that Cliff's arrest had occurred
on Western Shoshone and not U.S. land, she also took the case to
the Western Shoshone court system. That court ruled that crime
had been committed not by Cliff but by the U.S. by bringing BLM
agents and the sheriff's deputies into an area outside their jurisdiction. In the U.S. district court, Cliff was not so lucky. He was
sentenced and served nine months in jail. In *The Book of Elders*,
Carrie stated: "To this day I still believe it was wrong for the U.S.
to come in and throw their federal laws at us. It's obvious that the

court system doesn't work for indigenous people, no matter how right you are."

The Danns have the support of their nation. After Cliff's arrest, Western Shoshone Chief Raymond Yowell wrote several letters to President George Bush, demanding that the actions by the BLM be stopped. In the letter, Chief Yowell claimed that the U.S. government was violating human and civil rights and accused the government of genocide against the Western Shoshone people. He is quoted in the magazine *Indigenous Woman* as saying:

> *The situation in Crescent Valley is tense and the "danger of innocent blood being spilled is growing by the hour," Yowell told President Bush. "You have the executive power to stop this. Whether you have the courage to discipline your bureaucrats and order them to honor the Treaty [of Ruby Valley in 1863] made between two nations remains to be seen.*

The BLM, however, maintained that they were trying to avoid confrontation. "These horses are overgrazing and we have to do something about it," said BLM district manager Rodney Harris. He added that the horses could be claimed by their owners at the stockyards.

In 1993, Carrie and Mary Dann were awarded the Right Livelihood Award, an international "alternative Nobel Prize," supporting grassroots work that improves people's lives in practical ways. They were chosen by the award committee for "their courage and perseverance in asserting the right of indigenous people to their land."

As of 1996, the BLM had not tried again to remove stock from the disputed land. Department of the Interior officials are meeting with the Western Shoshone Nation to find a way to end the dispute. Carrie Dann and her sister Mary continue to fight for Western Shoshone land rights by grazing their cattle along with Western Shoshone cattle in the disputed area. Says Carrie Dann: "When you see your whole livelihood being stolen along with your land, it feels like the end of your life. The earth is part of us and we're a part of it."

MAE WILSON TSO

Navajo Land Rights Activist

(1937–)

Our Creator has placed us here on the land even before
the white man came. The Creator placed us without
boundaries. There was no such thing as Navajo or Hopi
land. . . . Our roots are way down deep and how can you
pull someone's culture, their way of life, their religion
out; when you try to do that by relocating the people,
our relatives, they suffer in many ways. When you have
relocated our relatives, you have taken them away from
who they are, what they are made of. . . .
                    —Mae Wilson Tso
                    (*The Wind Won't Know Me*, 1992)

It was April 4, 1986. Navajo grandmother Mae Wilson Tso sat with
her two sisters, Sara and Bessie, on Bessie's land. They had spread
sheepskins under a large juniper tree and were carding and spin-
ning wool into yarn. Soon they were joined by other Navajo
women. Sacks of food, enough to feed them for a week, surrounded the women as they worked.

The sisters had carefully selected their site; it was exactly in the path of a fence being built by the Hopi tribe under the guard of Bureau of Indian Affairs (BIA) police. Tso's son Sam and other traditional Navajo men stood nearby, the license plates of their trucks covered with signs that said BUZZ OFF. Hopi tribal officials watched and waited from a distance.

Finally, Lee Phillips, an attorney for the women through the Big Mountain Legal Defense/Offense Committee (BMLDOC), arrived to speak with Don Ami, head of the Hopi Department of Economic and Natural Resources. When Ami left, Tso lit a fire and started frying bread.

Toward the end of the day, word finally arrived from Ivan Sidney, the Hopi Tribal Chairman. He agreed to meet with the women in one week to talk about the land dispute issue. The women had been fighting for their traditional lands since 1977, when they learned their land had been given to the Hopi by the U.S. government. Determined not to relocate, the women knew their fight was far from over.

The Hopi Indians have lived in 14 villages in the Four Corners Area (where New Mexico, Arizona, Colorado, and Utah join) for over a millennium. The surrounding land contains several Hopi sacred sites and is used for grazing and farmland. The Navajo (called Dineh in their own language) settled on the land surrounding the Hopi villages about 500 years ago. Although their religions and cultures were quite different, the two groups lived peaceably, even intermarrying.

The Hopi were never removed from their villages. The Navajo, however, because of their frequent raids on Spanish and U.S. colonists, were captured by Kit Carson and forced to march to Fort Sumner, New Mexico. Mae's great grandmother was a part of this group of Navajo, but she escaped and returned to her people's land in Mosquito Springs. The Navajo who did not die were permitted to return to their traditional lands in 1868, with permission from the Hopi elders. They were totally unaware when

President Chester A. Arthur in 1882 drew boundaries to define a Hopi Reservation, a Navajo Reservation (which surrounded the Hopi land), and a Joint-Use Area in between. Mae's family's land was in the Joint-Use Area. The federal government also set up tribal councils for each nation, but the traditional peoples never accepted their leadership, preferring to listen to their elders/spiritual leaders as they had for centuries.

Navajo's lives are centered on their land and their sheep, which provide them with both food and clothing. When Mae was born in 1937, her mother, Blanche Wilson, buried her daughter's umbilical cord according to tradition in the ground near the sheep corral, as her mother and grandmother had done before her. Mae grew up speaking Navajo. She learned only a bit of English by attending Hardrock Mission School until she dropped out during the third grade. She has spent her entire life on the family's land and was given her own plot when she married and had a son.

Among the Navajo, land is considered a great gift from the Creator and is passed from mother to daughter. Their land is surrounded by four sacred mountains. Their one-room round houses, called hogans, are built to represent this land. As Tso explains:

> *The hogan has four main posts, which represent the four sacred mountains. . . . The top of the hogan represents the Father Sky. The bottom part is Mother Earth. Between these two are all living things. In the middle of the hogan is a place for the fire. In our ceremony, all our songs and prayers are within the hogan.*

When her first husband died, Mae married Askie Tso, and, according to custom, he came to live on Mae's land in Mosquito Springs. Together the couple had eight children. Mae cared for their sheep, prepared mutton stew and fry bread, and skillfully wove textiles to be sold to tourists. Because Askie worked for the Santa Fe Railroad, he was gone for several weeks at a time. The children helped with the sheep and attended school, where they became fluent in English. (Mae Tso's words have been translated from Navajo by Tso's oldest daughter, Betty.)

In the 1950s, the two tribal councils became anxious to clarify land rights so they could follow an energy development plan set up by the BIA. By this time, the Navajo population outnumbered the Hopi population. When federal laws upheld the rights of both tribes to the rich minerals in 1962, both tribal councils signed leases with Peabody Coal and other mining companies. Harvesting the land's minerals, however, was against the wishes of the traditional peoples of both tribes, who believe Mother Earth is a living body that is harmed by digging. The people also saw a sharp increase in disease among those men who worked in the mines.

In 1977, while Askie and Mae Tso were visiting relatives, a log cabin where part of their large family slept was hit by lightning, destroying its roof and one and one-half sides. Frightened, the three sons who were at home ran to their grandpa's house. That night, when Askie and Mae returned, the adults sat up all night, discussing what should be done, because, according to Navajo tradition, the family must abandon a structure hit by lightning. The entire family moved into the one-room hogan.

When the Tsos applied to the Navajo Tribe for building assistance, they were shocked to find that their land now belonged to the Hopi. A dispute between the two tribal councils over the Joint-Use Area in 1974 had resulted in a partitioning of the land. Because the Tsos lived in what was now the Hopi Partition Lands, they were told by law they could not rebuild and, along with 10,000 other Navajo and 1,000 Hopi, would be required to relocate by July 1986.

Shaken, the Tsos decided to rebuild on Askie's mother's land, which was in the Navajo partition. Each time they returned to their building site, however, they found that the walls of their new hogan had been torn down. They realized they were not welcome by Askie's relatives, who believed their own fragile survival on the desert land would be threatened by just one more family.

In the meanwhile, the Tsos joined with many other Navajo families who did not want to relocate. Since the Hopi did not seem to need the land, they reasoned it was really the minerals the Hopi Tribe wanted. In 1979, 64 elders of the Navajo Nation met at Big Mountain to sign a declaration:

Mae Tso cleans wool from her sheep in her one-room hogan. She will eventually use the wool to make rugs. (Ronnie Farley from *Women of the Native Struggle*)

The United States government and the Navajo Tribal Council have violated the sacred laws of the Dineh nations . . . [dividing] the indigenous people by boundaries or politics, Euro-American education, modernization, and Christianity. . . . Our Mother Earth is raped by the exploitation of coal, uranium, oil, natural gas and helium. . . . We speak for the winged beings, the four-legged beings, and those who have gone before us and the coming generation. We seek no changes in our livelihood because this natural life is our only known survival and it's our sacred law.

The Big Mountain Legal Defense/Offense Committee (BMLDOC) was formed in 1982, with an office in Flagstaff, Arizona. Named after an area in the disputed land, they began the work of raising money in an effort to get the relocation law repealed.

The Tsos decided to rebuild on their own land and chose a site north of their original house. They had only started building, however, when Navajo tribal officials told them to stop and, finally, came and tore down the new structure. Then Mae was tried in Tucson for violating the building restrictions. Confused and unable to understand English, Mae developed headaches and chest pains that lasted for several months. The family by this time included a daughter-in-law and a granddaughter, and all 13 of them were cramped into their original one-room hogan. It was 1983, six years after the fire, and the hogan itself was in need of repairs; its roof leaked and some of the logs were rotting.

Through the past six years, the idea of relocating had become unthinkable. Mae had seen relatives relocate to Flagstaff, Arizona, only to become homeless. Unfamiliar with taxes and utility bills, they had incurred debt, then lost their homes to dishonest real estate agents. The Tsos believed tragedy had come to these people because they had ignored their Navajo ways and moved from their lands.

The family moved into the damaged log cabin, tore down their hogan, and began to build another hogan at the same site. Officials from both the Navajo and Hopi tribes often parked their trucks nearby and watched them work, but did not stop them.

BIA police did come one day, however. They loaded the Tsoses' horses into trailers, and drove away. (The couple had refused to pay for livestock permits, Mae defiantly stating: "When the BIA shows us that they make the rains fall and the grass grow, then we'll consider paying them for livestock permits.")

Mae and Askie hopped into their truck and drove in front of the trailer, forcing the police to stop. Enraged, Mae began to shout at the police officers in Navajo, saying, "Why are you taking our horses?" Although the police were Indians, none of them was Navajo. According to Mae, one of the officers pushed her out of the way, and the trailer drove down the road. Frustrated, Mae grabbed a police officer by the hair and tried to kick him. Then she threw dirt into another officer's face. Two officers grabbed Mae, who continued to struggle until one of the officers hit her, and she blacked out.

She was taken to jail, but Tso refused to answer questions or even give her name. Although her eyeglasses were taken away, she refused to surrender her hair tie or put on jail clothes, which included pants. Tso was 46 years old and had never worn anything but the traditional Navajo flowing skirt and blouse. Later that day, Tso fainted; she woke up the next morning in the hospital. She had had a heart attack.

After recovering and being released from jail, Tso returned home to tend her sheep. Because they had run out of money, the family moved into the new hogan before it was completed. They blessed their new home by sprinkling its four corners with corn pollen in the traditional Navajo way. Tso fried bread in a small oven connected to a butane tank. Her Formica table and spring bed sat on a dirt floor. The family often ran out of firewood and water. Yet she was more determined than ever not to leave her land.

In the winter of 1986, Tso attended a meeting led by Peterson Zah, the new Navajo tribal chair. Zah respected the elders and wanted to help them. He had engineered many meetings with Arizona's congressional representative, Morris Udall, to find a compromise—a bill that could save their homes. The bill would allow most of the disputed land to be exchanged for other land, and the Navajo would pay the Hopi $300 million in coal revenues. Mae Tso, once a quiet woman who would never air her feelings publicly, stood to speak in favor of the bill, saying:

The struggle has been long and hard. The people are tired. I'm tired. Relocation has caused a lot of sickness, mentally and physically, among the people. And it has affected our children, because our children will not listen to us. They're going into drugs and alcohol. Maybe if this bill goes through, maybe the tribe can do something to help our young people.

Peterson Zah, however, lost the next election to Peter McDonald, whose main interest was selling the reservation's minerals to increase the wealth of the tribe. Then Morris Udall dropped his sponsorship of the bill. Nevertheless, the resistence movement became stronger. Navajo resisters met with traditional Hopi elders who supported their cause. Attorneys for the BMLDOC increased their effort to get the relocation law repealed.

Mae Tso's life was changing against her will. To plead her case, she had consented to traveling across the country to help gain support for the BMLDOC. The committee had been quite success-

Mae Tso, center, stands in front of her hogan with (from left to right) her grandmother Jenny Manybeads, her mother Blanche Wilson, her daughter Betty, and her granddaughter Fiona (Earl's daughter). (Ronnie Farley from Women of the Native Struggle)

ful in garnering support nationwide and had even opened additional offices in Atlanta, Kansas City, St. Louis, and Washington, D.C. At a rally in Los Angeles in 1986, actor Jon Voight and several singers including Buffy Sainte-Marie denounced the relocation plan. The Grateful Dead even donated the proceeds from one of their rock concerts.

Mae's absences were hard on her family. Askie especially felt abandoned and was jealous of the attention Mae was receiving. One day in the spring he returned home from his job and threw Mae out of the house. "Never come back," he told her. Mae lived with her sister Bessie until she and Askie reconciled two months later. Their son, Earl, began to take over some of the traveling demands.

Then the BIA started building fences on the disputed land to "manage" the range. To the traditional Navajo, even planting fence posts and driving vehicles over their land was dishonoring Mother Earth. They believed the BIA was harassing them. Meanwhile, the Hopi Tribal Council had begun to move stock pens and build livestock ponds on the disputed land.

After their fence protest, Mae Tso and her sisters decided not to attend the scheduled meeting with Hopi Tribal Chair Ivan Sidney. Sidney said he would only meet with two representatives, and the women did not believe two of them could speak for the entire group. All the women attended a subsequent relocation meeting, but Sidney refused to discuss the fence issue. The Navajo scored a victory a short time later, however, when the federal government ordered Hopi law enforcement and fence crews to avoid sacred burial grounds and halt the ongoing harassment.

On June 3, Mae Tso attended an International Indian Treaty Conference at Big Mountain sponsored by the American Indian Movement (AIM). Their purpose was to gather information on the land dispute to be submitted to the United Nations Commission on Human Rights and the Working Group on Indigenous Populations. At the meeting, an announcement was made that the Hopi Tribal Council had dropped all charges against Mae Tso for her resistance over removal of her horses. Tso jumped up and down and hugged the Navajo women who congratulated her. Later, the women took the stage to sing songs about their land and animals.

In July, Mae Tso was present at an AIM-sponsored sundance at Big Mountain. She joined about 300 other protestors in a three-mile walk from the camp to the partition fence. Navajo elder Roberta Blackgoat, age 69, carried a sign that said, "The Creator is the only one who's going to relocate us." Tso walked beside her, carrying the American flag upside down. When questioned about her actions by a group of Navajo veterans, Tso explained she was doing so because the government had made her feel worthless by taking away everything she held dear. Then she reminded the men that Indians have their own flag—the eagle—that flies without any poles or staff or any kind of assistance.

By now, all Navajo willing to relocate had done so. Two hundred Navajo families remained in the Hopi partition, unwilling to move. In 1988, BMLDOC attorney Lee Phillips, with the support of the National Council of Churches, filed a suit in Federal District Court alleging that the relocation of the Navajo violated their First Amendment rights to worship. Although a federal court ruled that the law does not protect the exercise of religion that is tied to a particular location, a court of appeals in 1991 ordered negotiations between the two tribes to settle the dispute without forced relocation.

In 1993, the Hopi Tribal Council approved a plan called the Agreement in Principle (AIP) that would allow Navajo to apply for permission to live on the land in 75-year increments. The Navajo in question, however, refused to accept Hopi jurisdiction of their land and opposed the omission of a religious freedom clause that would recognize their sacred relationship to their homeland. Three different proposals followed, but none was agreeable to all parties. Navajo president Albert Hale finally signed the original agreement, believing it was the best settlement the Navajo could hope for.

Mae Tso continues to live on her land and care for her sheep. She and other resisters have stated they will refuse to apply for leases and will defend against eviction with gunfire, if necessary. The AIP was passed by Congress and signed by President Bill Clinton in October 1996, but the deadline for signing the leases was extended until a fairness hearing could be held in a federal court in Phoenix.

JOHN E. ECHOHAWK

Pawnee Attorney and Reformer

Executive Director of the Native
American Rights Fund (NARF)

(1945–)

> The salvation for the tribes was right there in the law
> books—in the federal treaties and promises. They were
> protected by the Constitution of the United States—it
> was right there.
>   —John E. Echohawk
>   (*The Denver Post Magazine*, October 16, 1994)

When the federal government decided on a policy of tribal
termination in the early 1950s, the first tribe to be terminated, or
forced to assimilate, was the Menominee of Wisconsin. By the time
the effects of termination were proven to be disastrous, and the
Menominee wanted their status as a tribe and the provisions of
their treaty with the U.S. reinstated, John Echohawk had just
graduated from law school. It was 1970, and he was working for

a new organization, the Native American Rights Fund (NARF). Echohawk lent his help to the efforts of Ada Deer, a Menominee who led the restoration movement for her people. He and other NARF attorneys served as Ada Deer's legal advisors as she prepared to speak on the issue before Congress. After two years of lobbying, Congress realized it had made a mistake and passed the Menominee Restoration Act, which reinstated the Menominee as a federally recognized tribe. In 1973, President Richard Nixon signed the bill into law.

"When the case came, we knew it would be a difficult case," said Echohawk. "U.S. policy in the 1960s was to ignore or overlook treaties," he said. Calling their success a "historic point in Indian affairs," Echohawk was "honored and pleased to participate" in the case.

Since 1970, John Echohawk has continued to work for NARF to help Indians claim their rights not only to tribal existence, but for protection of tribal natural resources, promotion of human rights, accountability of the government to Native Americans, and the development of Indian law. Although soft-spoken about his own achievements, he radiates a charismatic firmness when fighting for Indian rights. In 1988, 1991, and again in 1994, he was selected by the *National Law Journal* as one of the 100 most influential lawyers in the United States. (Each selection is for three years.)

The Echohawk family line is long and distinguished. John Echohawk's great-grandfather was a Pawnee scout for the U.S. Cavalry during the 1870s. Although he was a great warrior, Echo Hawk never spoke of his own achievements, but members of his tribe spoke proudly of him. The honored scout was given the name Echo Hawk because their praises were like an echo.

During the late 1800s, the Pawnee were forced from their Nebraskan homelands to reservations in Oklahoma. Their numbers dropped from 25,000 to only 750 persons. Echo Hawk's grandson, Brummett Echo Hawk, was born in Oklahoma in 1922. He became a noted artist who painted scenes of Native American events, such as his *Trail of Tears*, which shows the forced removal of the

John E. Echohawk.

Cherokee from the South to Oklahoma during the 1830s. Brummett also was a writer, actor, and comic strip artist.

Brummett's brother Ernest is John Echohawk's father. Ernest attended a government boarding school until the sixth grade, when he was among the first group of Indian children in Oklahoma to attend public school. He attended Albuquerque High School and went to the University of New Mexico on a football scholarship. He became a land surveyor and worked in the oil fields. Later, he owned a surveying company.

Ernest married a white neighbor, Jane Conrad. Jane convinced Ernest to change the family name from Echo Hawk to one word, Echohawk, as she was tired of being called Mrs. Hawk. A close-knit family, the couple had two daughters and four sons. John Echohawk was born in 1945 in Albuquerque, New Mexico. Of the three brothers who followed, two became attorneys. His brother Larry EchoHawk was a candidate for governor of Idaho in 1994.

The family grew up in Farmington, a small town in the north-west corner of New Mexico, where they attended public school. Both parents stressed the importance of education and enforced an 11 P.M. curfew for their children. John played football and was student body president in high school. Martin Luther King, Jr., served as an inspiration to him, in part because the civil rights movement of the 1960s opened greater opportunities for Indians. He won an academic scholarship to the University of New Mexico in Albuquerque, where he was the first graduate of a special program to train Indian lawyers. He married Kathryn Martin in 1965 and had two children, Christopher and Sarah.

Echohawk received a B.A. degree in 1967 and graduated from the University of New Mexico's School of Law in 1970. At that time, there were only about 20 Indian lawyers throughout the country. In law school, John learned about laws and rights pertaining to American Indians. He became dedicated to the idea of being an attorney for Indian rights, believing "a law doesn't do any good until it is enforced, so we [Indians] had to learn the legal process." While in law school, Echohawk cofounded the American Indian Law Students Association.

In 1970, John Echohawk became one of the founders of the Native American Rights Fund (NARF). Seeing a need to have a central national perspective for the practice of Federal Indian law, NARF was formed as a pilot project in California, funded by the Ford Foundation, and assisted by the California Indian Legal Services and the legal academic community.

To be closer to "Indian country," in 1971 NARF moved to Boulder, Colorado, where Echohawk and other staff members work to enforce laws nationwide that pertain to Indians. As a nonprofit organization supported mostly by grants and individual contributions, it nevertheless grew quickly, establishing offices in Washington, D.C., and Anchorage, Alaska. NARF supports Indian nations as sovereign governments, separate from the U.S. government, while recognizing that the federal government has a legal responsibility through its treaties to assist Indian nations. In a 1995 interview for *Flatirons*, Echohawk stated:

The treaties are all in the law books. Tribes ceded vast areas that are now the United States of America in return for the protection and assistance of their people and their needs. These treaties are the law of the land, and that hasn't changed. As far as tribes are concerned, the U.S. can't do enough toward fulfilling those promises.

From 1972 to 1973 Echohawk served as NARF's deputy director. It was during this time that the American Indian Movement (AIM) was investigating Oglala Lakota Raymond Yellow Thunder's murder in South Dakota (See chapter 5). NARF arranged to have another pathologist examine Yellow Thunder's body, and John Echohawk traveled to Gordon, Nebraska, to be present at this second exam.

Echohawk was named executive director of NARF in 1973 and vice executive director in 1975. He was reappointed executive director of NARF in 1977 and, as of 1996, still holds that position. Vine Deloria, Jr., another attorney and leader in Indian law, speaks well of John Echohawk:

NARF is located in a large fraternity house near the University of Colorado in Boulder. After purchasing the trashed building in 1971, NARF transformed it to its present Spanish-style stucco look. (© Thorney Lieberman)

John can lay claim to the title of the most stable Indian organizational executive. With remarkable patience and wisdom, John has led an occasionally controversial organization on a path of steady and sustained growth unmatched in Indian history.

One of NARF's most critical issues, according to Echohawk, is the preservation of tribes as "governmental entities with all the power and authority that governmental status entails." They help tribes not formally recognized by the federal government gain recognition as sovereign governments and assist federally recognized tribes to gain the power to regulate internal affairs and activities on their reservations.

Through their work, U.S. courts have upheld tribal rights to tax oil and gas activities on Indian land held in trust—or protected—by the U.S. government. In 1976, for example, when the Army Corps of Engineers in Nebraska condemned Winnebago reservation land along the Missouri River for a flood control project, NARF successfully argued in court that the corps could not do so because of the Winnebago's treaty with the U.S., even though the corps had the right to condemn nonreservation land.

Another important issue is the protection of tribal natural resources such as land. In 1980, NARF succeeded in getting Maine to return 300,000 acres and to pay $27 million to the Passamaquody. It was the largest return of land to Indians in U.S. history. To win the case, NARF first had to sue the U.S. attorney general to force him to press the case. By law, the federal government is required to represent Indian tribes, but the United States often neglects this duty when one of its agencies—such as the Bureau of Reclamation—wants Indian land for such projects as building dams.

In addition to land rights, water rights also are often disputed. In 1908, the Supreme Court established that Indian tribes have reserved water rights and are entitled to sufficient water for present and future needs. As farming and other industries grow on reservations, their need for water has become greater. NARF has been involved in many of the 50 lawsuits in the Western states to define the exact amount of water to which each tribe is entitled.

NARF also helps tribes gain the right to hunt and fish in traditional areas, both on and off reservations, according to their treaty provisions. Dams built in the early 1900s on the White River in the state of Washington, for example, eliminated salmon habitat above and below the dam. NARF helped the Muckleshoot Tribe seek compensation for damages as well as measures to restore the tribe's fishery.

NARF works to uphold the religious rights of American Indians in accordance with the First Amendment, which states that Congress "shall make no law respecting an establishment of religion, or prohibiting the free exercise thereof . . ." Although the American Indian Religious Freedom Act was passed by Congress in 1978, the Supreme Court has ruled that it does not protect sacred sites on federal land formerly owned by tribes from being bulldozed. Nor does it allow use of the cactus plant peyote in Native American religious ceremonies or require museums to return native religious items and human remains to the Indian people. Regarding these decisions, Echohawk stated for *Flatirons*: "The court was wrong. They changed the rules on us. Now everybody has religious freedom except Native American people."

In 1990, NARF helped to pass a bill requiring the repatriation (return) of native religious items and remains to the tribes. Another bill was passed in 1994 that allows peyote to be used legally in ceremonies conducted by the Native American Church. In an October 1994 article he wrote for *Buzzworm's Earth Journal*, Echohawk concluded:

> *In reviewing the plight of Native Americans then and now, we can only regret the enormous loss of our cultural and environmental heritage as a result of government oppression of tribal religious beliefs and practices. The challenge to our generation, however, is to preserve what little is left for present and future generations.*

John Echohawk also serves on several other boards including the American Indian Resources Institute, the Association on American Indian Affairs, and the National Center for American Indian Enterprise Development. He was a member of President Clinton's transition team in 1992, helping that administration reshape the Bureau of Indian Affairs (BIA). Although President Clinton offered him an administrative post, he declined it, preferring to continue his work with NARF. Echohawk has received numerous awards, including the Distinguished Service Award from Americans for Indian Opportunity (AIO). A member of the Democratic Party, he enjoys skiing and fishing as well as visits from his granddaughter.

Awards Received by John E. Echohawk

Distinguished Service Award, Americans for Indian Opportunity, 1982
Friendship Award, White Buffalo Council, 1983
President's Indian Service Award, National Congress of American Indians, 1984
Annual Indian Achievement Award, Indian Council Fire, 1987
One of the 100 Most Influential Attorneys in the U.S., *National Law Journal*, 1988, 1991, 1994
Spirit of Excellence Award, American Bar Association, 1996

Boards and Committees
American Indian Policy Review Committee, U.S. Senate, 1976–77
American Indian Lawyer Training Program, 1975–present
Association on American Indian Affairs, 1980–present
National Committee on Responsible Philanthropy, 1981–present
Independent Sector, 1986–92
Natural Resources Defense Council, 1988–present
National Center Enterprise Development, 1988–present
Transition Team for Interior Department, 1992–93
Keystone Center, 1993–present
Environmental and Energy Study Institute, 1994–present

Memberships
Colorado Indian Bar Association
American Indian Bar Association

SELECTED ANNOTATED BIBLIOGRAPHY

General Sources

Avery, Susan, and Linda Skinner. *Extraordinary American Indians*. Chicago: Childrens Press, 1992. Excellent source of biographies as well as AIM and Wounded Knee II information for young people. See articles listed under specific subjects below.

Benedek, Emily. *The Wind Won't Know Me: A History of the Navajo-Hopi Land Dispute*. New York: Alfred Knopf, 1992. Thorough and personal account of the effects of relocation on the Navajo by a *Newsweek* reporter, as well as background information on both the Hopi and the Navajo. Includes biographical chapters on Mae Wilson Tso.

Champagne, Duane. *Native America: Portrait of the Peoples*. Detroit: Visible Ink Press, 1994. Excellent source of biographies on Anna Mae Aquash, Dennis Banks, Gertrude Simmons Bonnin, Vine Deloria, Jr., LaDonna Harris, and Russell Means.

Edmunds, David R. *American Indian Leaders: Studies in Diversity*. Lincoln: University of Nebraska Press, 1980. Specific articles listed under subjects below.

Fixico, Donald L. *Urban Indians*. Series: Indians of North America. New York: Chelsea House, 1991. Describes the conditions of urban Indians. Has some AIM information.

Gridley, Marion Eleanor. *Contemporary American Indian Leaders*. New York: Dodd, Mead, 1972. Specific articles listed under subjects below.

Jaimes, Annette M. *The State of Native America: Genocide, Colonization, and Resistance*. Boston: South End Press, 1992. Contains no biographies, but discusses topics that pertain to Indians by issue. Difficult reading.

Johnson, Sandy. *The Book of Elders: The Life Stories of Great American Indians*. San Francisco: HarperSanFrancisco, 1994. Provides interesting life stories as told to the author. Great photos. See articles listed under specific subjects below.

Trimble, Stephen. *The People: Indians of the American Southwest*. Santa Fe: School of American Research Press, 1993. Complete history that includes information about the Navajo-Hopi Land Dispute and two pages on the Echohawks.

Film

How the West Was Lost, produced by Jim Burger. Bethesda, Md.: Discovery Enterprises Group, 1993. A collection of three videocassettes that documents through interviews and photographs the devastating effects of the westward expansion on Indians.

The Way West, produced by Steeplechase Films. Newton, N.J.: Shanachie Entertainment Corp., 1995. Four videocassettes (360 min.) that tell the story of the gold rush through the end of the Indian Wars from both sides.

The West, directed by Stephen Ives, written by Geoffrey C. Wood and Dayton Duncan. Alexandria, Va.: PBS Video, 1996. Nine videocassettes with black-and-white sequences: v. 1. The People; v. 2. Empire upon the Trails; v. 3. The Speck of the Future; v. 4. Death Runs Riot; v. 5. The Grandest Enterprise under God; v. 6. Fight No More Forever; v. 7. The Geography of Hope; v. 8. Ghost Dance; v. 9. One Sky above Us.

The American Indian Movement (AIM)

Avery, Susan, and Linda Skinner. *Extraordinary American Indians*. Chicago: Childrens Press, 1992. Excellent source of biographies as well as AIM and Wounded Knee II information for young people. See articles listed under specific subjects below.

Brand, Joanna. *The Life and Death of Anna Mae Aquash*. Toronto: James Lorimer & Company, 1978. A complete biography of an AIM member whose death shortly after Wounded Knee II has never been solved.

Lyman, Stanley David. *Wounded Knee 1973*. Lincoln: University of Nebraska Press, 1991. Personal account of Wounded Knee II from the point of view of the Bureau of Indian Affairs (BIA) superintendent at the Pine Ridge Reservation.

Matthiessen, Peter. *In the Spirit of Crazy Horse*. Viking Press, 1983. Most thorough and controversial book on Wounded Knee II, its aftermath, and the government's "persecution" of Leonard Peltier, written by an AIM sympathizer.

Stern, Kenneth S. *Loud Hawk: The United States versus the American Indian Movement*. Norman: University of Oklahoma Press, 1994. The author was a student attorney working on the trial of Dennis Banks and other AIM members who were arrested in Oregon in 1976.

U.S. Senate Subcommittee, *Revolutionary Activities Within the United States: The American Indian Movement*, Sept. 1976. The story told from the government's point of view.

Voices from Wounded Knee, 1973: In the Words of the Participants. Rooseveltown, NY: *Akwesasne Notes*, 1974. A national Indian newsletter produced by the Six Nations offers a collection of documents, quotations, and transcripts from both sides of the conflict.

Film

Incident at Oglala. Carolco Home Video, 1991. Narrated by Robert Redford, it tells the story of the shoot-out between AIM members and the FBI on the Pine Ridge Reservation in 1975 and the subsequent arrest, trial, and conviction of Leonard Peltier.

Introduction

Avery, Susan, and Linda Skinner. "Tribal Termination and Self-Determination," *Extraordinary American Indians*, Chicago: Childrens Press, 1992. Understandable explanations of these two issues.

Gertrude Simmons Bonnin

Avery, Susan, and Linda Skinner. "Gertrude Simmons Bonnin." *Extraordinary American Indians*. Chicago: Childrens Press, 1992. A short but helpful biography.

Bonnin, Gertrude. *Oklahoma's Poor Rich Indians: An Orgy of Graft and Exploitation of the Five Civilized Tribes — Legalized Robbery*. Philadelphia: Office of the Indian Rights Association, 1924. The complete report written by Bonnin.

Champagne, Duane. *Native America: Portrait of the Peoples*. Detroit: Visible Ink Press, 1994. Short biography about this Native American leader.

Fisher, Dexter. "Introduction: Zitkala-Sa: The Evolution of a Writer." *American Indian Stories* by Zitkala-Sa. First Bison printing, 1985. Several pages of interesting biography on Gertrude Bonnin.

Clinton Rickard

Graymont, Barbara, ed. *Fighting Tuscarora: The Autobiography of Chief Clinton Rickard*. Syracuse: Syracuse University Press, 1973. A complete account written with the help of a professor from Nyack University in New York.

LaDonna Harris

Avery, Susan, and Linda Skinner. *Extraordinary American Indians*. Chicago: Childrens Press, 1992. Short but excellent source.

Champagne, Duane. *Native America: Portrait of the Peoples*. Detroit: Visible Ink Press, 1994. Short biography.

Gordon-McCutchan, R.C. *The Taos Indians and the Battle for Blue Lake*. Santa Fe: Red Crane Books, 1991. The book tells the story of the Taos Indians' legal fight to get their sacred lake back, with a bit of information on LaDonna Harris and her role.

Gridley, Marion Eleanor. "LaDonna Harris," *Contemporary American Indian Leaders*. New York: Dodd, Mead, 1972. Short biography.

Morris, Terry. "LaDonna Harris: A Woman Who Gives a Damn." *Redbook*, February 1970. This article gives lots of interesting information about Harris's childhood and early career.

Vine Deloria, Jr.

Avery, Susan, and Linda Skinner. "The Delorias." *Extraordinary American Indians*. Chicago: Childrens Press, 1992. Short but excellent source of information on the Deloria family.

Champagne, Duane. *Native America: Portrait of the Peoples*. Detroit: Visible Ink Press, 1994. A short biography about this American Indian leader.

Deloria, Vine, Jr. *Custer Died for Your Sins*. New York: Macmillan, 1969. An Indian manifesto—a book that explains Indians to non-Indians.

———. *God Is Red*. New York: Grosset & Dunlap, 1973. An easy-to-read but searing view of America and Christianity from the Indians' point of view.

———. *Red Earth, White Lies*. New York: Scribner, 1996. Deloria attempts to show that American Indians' oral history regarding their origins is scientifically more accurate than the theory that they crossed over the Bering Strait.

Gridley, Marion Eleanor. "Vine Deloria, Jr." *Contemporary American Indian Leaders*. New York: Dodd, Mead, 1972. A short but helpful biography.

Dennis Banks

Avery, Susan, and Linda Skinner. *Extraordinary American Indians*. Chicago: Childrens Press, 1992. Gives a bit of information about Banks under the "AIM" and "Wounded Knee" articles.

Champagne, Duane. *Native America: Portrait of the Peoples*. Detroit: Visible Ink Press, 1994. Short biography plus an introduction written by Dennis Banks.

Current Biography Yearbook, 1992. Several pages of biography on Dennis Banks.

Sacred Run Newsletter, PO Box 315, Newport, KY 41071. Give updated information about the activities of the Sacred Run Foundation.

Russell Means

Champagne, Duane. *Native America: Portrait of the Peoples*. Detroit: Visible Ink Press, 1994. Short biography.

Means, Russell. *Where White Men Fear to Tread: The Autobiography of Russell Means*. New York: St. Martin's Press, 1995. This 550-page book is interesting because it is well written, with the help of writer Marvin J. Wolf, and full of opinions.

Plummer, William. "Hearing His Own Drum: Activist Russell Means Dances with Hollywood." *People Weekly*, v38, Oct 12, 92, p. 63(4). This feature talks about Means's switch to an acting career.

Anna Mae Aquash

Brand, Joanna. *The Life and Death of Anna Mae Aquash*. Toronto: James Lorimer & Company, 1978. This book gives interesting details about Aquash's childhood as well as Wounded Knee II and Aquash's work with AIM. It also deals with her murder, mulling over the motives and possible suspects.

Champagne, Duane. *Native America: Portrait of the Peoples*. Detroit: Visible Ink Press, 1994.

Film

Annie Mae—Brave Hearted Woman. Written/produced/directed by Lan Brookes Ritz. Hollywood: Downtown Bird Productions, Inc., 1988. (213) 851-8928. This 16 mm film was done as a tribute to Aquash and includes interviews with people who knew her, as well as excerpts from her letters.

Carrie Dann

Johnson, Sandy. "Carrie Dann." *The Book of Elders: The Life Stories of Great American Indians*. San Francisco: HarperSanFrancisco, 1994.

Farley, Ronnie. *Women of the Native Struggle: Portraits and Testimony of Native American Women*. New York: Orion Books, 1993. Includes photographs of Carrie and Mary Dann and quotations by Carrie Dann.

Taliman, Valerie. "Feds Seize Western Shoshone Livestock!" *Indigenous Woman*, December, 1992. A journalistic report written soon after the BLM seized the Dann livestock.

Western Shoshone Defense Project Newsletter, PO Box 211106, Crescent Valley, NV 89821. Gives updates on the Dann case and other projects of the WSDP.

Film

Broken Treaty at Battle Mountain. New York: Cinnamon Productions, 1974. A documentary about land transfers and treaties with the Western Shoshone. Motion picture 1974; videocassette 1984.

Mae Wilson Tso

Benedek, Emily. *The Wind Won't Know Me: A History of the Navajo-Hopi Land Dispute*. New York: Alfred Knopf, 1992. Thorough and personal account of the efforts of Mae Tso and other Navajo to remain on their traditional lands.

Farley, Ronnie. *Women of the Native Struggle: Portraits and Testimony of Native American Women*. New York: Orion Books, 1993. Includes photographs of Mae Tso.

Trimble, Stephen. *The People: Indians of the American Southwest*. Santa Fe: School of American Research Press, 1993. Complete history that includes the beginnings of the Hopi-Navajo land dispute.

"Warning from Black Mesa," *Creation*. January/February 1987. Vol. 2 #6. Hopi traditional religious leaders speak out against the relocation.

Film

Broken Rainbow. Direct Cinema, 1987. Documentary about relocation of Navajo to tract homes in Arizona towns.

John Echohawk

Avery, Susan, and Linda Skinner. *Extraordinary American Indians.* Chicago: Childrens Press, 1992. Short but excellent source of information on the Echohawks.

Ditmer, Joanne. "Flying High: The Echohawks: Portrait of an American Family." *The Denver Post Magazine*, October 16, 1994. The article features the Echohawk family, with quotes from John Echohawk.

Echohawk, John E. "Native Americans: Then and Now," *Buzzworm's Earth Journal*, January/February, 1994. John Echohawk explains earth-based religion and the need for a new law to secure religious freedom for Native Americans.

Patterson, Eric. "A Time of Reckoning: Courtroom Warriors are Gaining Ground for Native Americans," *Flatirons: The Boulder Magazine*. Spring/Summer, 1995. An in-depth article about the Native American Rights Fund (NARF) located in Boulder, Colorado.

Trimble, Stephen. *The People: Indians of the American Southwest*. Santa Fe: School of American Research Press, 1993. Two pages on the Echohawks.

Index

Boldface type indicates main readings. *Italic* type indicates illustrations.

A

activities of daily life   3, 16, 26, 72, 80

Agnew, Spiro   30

Agreement in Principle (AIP)   87

American Indian Ambassadors Program   33

American Indian Declaration of Independence   39

American Indian Magazine   9–10

American Indian Movement (AIM)   47–69

    and Big Mountain land dispute   86–87

    founding of   49

    and Russell Means   59–64

American Indian Religious Freedom Resolution   39

Americans for Indian Opportunity (AIO)   24

Andrus, Cecil   73

animal extinction   45

Anishinabe nation   49

Aquash, Anna Mae   48, **65–69**

    as AIM fund-raiser   67–69

    early years   65

    murder of   69

Army Corps of Engineers   93

Arthur, President Chester   80

assimilation   8–9, 36. *See also* Society of American Indians

astronomy. *See* star knowledge

B

Bad Heart Bull, Wesley   52

Banks, Dennis   48, **49–58**, 59

    and AIM   49–51

    and Anna Mae Aquash burial   69

    and BIA takeover   51–52

    and Plymouth, Mass. confrontation   51

    and Wounded Knee   52–56

Bellecourt, Clyde   48, 51, 59

Bering Strait migration theory   45

BIA headquarters takeover   32

Big Mountain

    declaration and defense committee   82–83, 85–86

Bissonnette, Pedro   48

Black Hills, South Dakota   51

    and land rights   54

    occupation of   63

Blue Lake issue   31

    and Vine Deloria, Jr.   41

    LaDonna Harris involvement in   24–25

Bonnin, Gertrude Simmons   **1–12**

    education   3–6

    literary career   7

    as writer and editor   9–10

Bonnin, Captain Raymond   7

Book of Elders, The   76

border crossing issue   13, 19–20

    Border Crossing Celebration   14, 20

    Indian opposition to   20

Boston Indian Council (BIC)   65

Brown, Governor Jerry   56

Bureau of Indian Affairs (BIA)   7, 94

    activism against   30–31

    and Gertrude Bonnin   10

    and LaDonna Harris   32

Indian leadership of 11
and Navajo-Hopi land
   dispute 78–79
opposition to 9
at Pine Ridge 48
suit against 55
takeover of 52
Bureau of Land Management
   70
   and Carrie Dann case 72–77

C

Carlisle Indian School 5
Carter, President Jimmy 33
Cayuga tribe 14, 22
ceremonial trees 73–74
ceremonies 72. *See also* Indian
   culture
Chiefs' Council 18
Chippewa nation 49
churches. *See* National Council of
   Churches
citizenship issue 10, 11
   Citizenship Act 18–19
   Indian opposition to 18
civil rights 77
Clinton, President Bill 33, 94
   and AIP bill 87
Collier, John
   and Indian Reorganization
      Act 11–12
Comanche tribe 25
computer technology 33
Coolidge, President Calvin 20
Council for Energy Resource
   Tribes (CERT) 32
court advocacy program 50
Custer, South Dakota confronta-
   tion 52
   legal results of 56
   and Russell Means 62
Custer Died for Your Sins 36, 38

D

Dakota tribe 36
Dann, Carrie **70–77**
   early years 71–72
Dann, Clifford 71, 76
Dann, Mary 72, 75
Dann Defense Project 75
Deer, Ada 12
Deloria, Vine, Jr. **35–46,** 92
   awards received by *46t*
   career milestones 42
   early years 35–37
   education and career 37–38
   later publications of 43–44
   literary career 38–41
   teaching career of 44
Deloria family
   as prominent Sioux 36
democracy 39
Department of Agriculture 31
Department of Energy 31
Department of the Interior 11
Deskaheh (Chief) 19
"Dick Cavett Show"
   and Vine Deloria, Jr. 41
Dineh tribe. *See* Navajo
discipline, Comanche 26–27

E

eagle symbol 87
earth reverence 80, 81, 86
Eastman, Charles 2
Echo Hawk, Brummett 89
Echo Hawk, Ernest 90
Echohawk, John **88–95**
   awards received by *95t*
   early years 91
Ecoffey, Robert 69
education issue 11, 27
   choices for young Indians 4, 5
   Indian rights to 18
elder conferences 45
Environmental Protection Agency

and Indian policy   31
Everett Report   18
Every Child by Two   33

F

family values
    in Comanche tradition   26–27
FBI
    and Anna Mae Aquash death
        69
    and Pine Ridge confrontation
        68
    at Wounded Knee   48
    and Wounded Knee trial
        56, 62
federal jurisdiction   22. *See also*
    Bureau of Indian Affairs; FBI;
    Supreme Court
Fighting Tuscarora   15
fishing rights issue   93
    and migration theory   45
    and Vine Deloria, Jr.   41
Ford, President Gerald   32
Fort Laramie Treaty of 1868   42,
    53, 54, 61
Freemasonry   17

G

General Federation of Women's
    Clubs   2, 10
Ghent, Treaty of   19
Ghost Dance massacre   5
Ghost Dance religion   4
Ghost Dance at Wounded Knee   61
God Is Red   42
Goon Squad   68
    and Anna Mae Aquash death
        69
    at Wounded Knee   48
Grateful Dead 86
Graymont, Barbara   28

H

hair length, Sioux   4
Harris, LaDonna   12, **24–34**
    activist career of   30–32
    awards received by   *34t*
    early education   27
    early years   26–27
    marriage to Fred   28
    political career of   32–33
hogans   80
Hoover, President Herbert   11
Hopi land dispute   79
humor, in AIM   60
hunting rights   45, 93

I

Immigration Act   19
immunization programs   33
Indian Child Welfare Act   39
Indian culture   12, 36–37, 80
    and aging   75
    better understanding of   45
    and the earth   80, 81, 86
    and hair length   4
    and humor   60
    and mining   81
Indian Defense League of America
    (IDLA)   13–14, 19
Indian humor   38–39
Indian manifesto   36
INDIANnet   33
Indian Reorganization Act   12
Indian science   44
Institute for the Development of
    Indian Law   41
Institute of American Indian Arts
    Board   33
integration   28
international understanding   33
International Women's Year   32

J

Jay Treaty of 1794   14, 19

Johnson, President Lyndon   30

K
Kinzua Dam   23
Kiowa–Comanche–Apache Reservation   26

L
land control   25
    in New York State   18, 23
    Oklahoma   10–11
land dispute
    inter–tribal   79, 81–84
land ownership
    matrilineal   80
land reclamation   12
land reverence   80, 81, 86
    and religious faith   42–43
land rights
    Carrie Dann struggle for   70
    Deloria's activism for   38
    struggle for   72–77
land settlements   31
Last of the Mohicans, The (film)   64
Libertarian Party   64
livestock seizure   75–76, 83
"The Longest Walk"   57

M
Maine land case   93
Masons. *See* Freemasonry
Mayflower II confrontation   51, 59, 67
Means, Russell   48, **58–64**
    and Wounded Knee   54
    acting career   64
Menominee tribe   56, 88–89
Merriam Commission   2, 10
Micmac reservation   65
migration theory   45. *See also* border crossing issue
military service   10
mining   81

Miskito Indians   64
missionary schooling   3–4
Model Urban Indian Centers
    Project   41
Mohawk tribe   14
Montezuma, Carlos   2
Muckleshoot Tribe   94

N
National Committee Against
    Discrimination in Housing   33
National Congress of American
    Indians (NCAI)   37–38
National Council for Indian
    Opportunity (NCIO)   25, 30, 31
National Council of American
    Indians (NCAI)   1, 11
National Council of Churches
    50–51, 59
    and relocation protest   87
National Indian Housing Council
    33
National Institute for Women of
    Color   33
National Organization for
    Women   32
National Organization on Fetal
    Alcohol Syndrome   33
National Urban League   33
National Women's Political
    Caucus   32
nationhood   48. *See also* entries at
    tribal
Native American Rights Fund
    (NARF)   88–89, 91
Navajo land dispute   79
Niagra Falls area   14–15
Nicaragua   64
Nichol, Judge Alfred
    and Wounded Knee trial   56, 62
Nixon, President Richard   25, 30, 89

and AIM 52
nonviolence 64
Northwest Ordinance 73

O

Of Utmost Faith 41
Oglala Lakota Indians 47
Oglala Sioux Legal Rights
  Foundation 41
Ohiya 7
Ojibwa nation 49
Oklahoma
    activism in 28
    Oklahomans for Indian
      Opportunity 28–29, 31
Oneida tribe 14
Onondaga tribe 14
origins 45
Ouray Reservation 7

P

Passamaquody land case 93
Pawnee tribe 88–90
Pax World Foundation 33
Peace Corps 30
Peace Pipe Project 30
peyote issue 11, 94
    in religious ceremony 27
Pine Ridge Reservation 47
    confrontation 60, 68
    and Russell Means 64
Plymouth, Massachusetts confron-
    tation 51, 59, 67
Pocahantas 64
police brutality 41, 51
    AIM efforts to reduce 49–50
prejudice 27. *See also* racism
property rights 11

R

racism 27, 51
    and AIM 50
    in South Dakota 68

reclamation, land 12
Red Earth, White Lies 45
Red Man in the New World Drama 41
religion 61. *See also* earth
    reverence 42
religious rights 94
relocation issue 83, 87
    Hopi and Navajos 81
    Pawnee tribe 89
repatriation rights 94
Rickard, Beulah 22
Rickard, Clinton **13–23**
    first marriage of 16–17
    military service of 16
    second marriage of 18
Rickard, Elizabeth 20
Rickard, George 15
Right Livelihood Award 77
rites. *See* ceremonies; Indian culture
Roosevelt, Franklin D. 22

S

Sacred Run Foundation 58
Sainte-Marie, Buffy 86
Sandinistas 64
Santa Ana Pueblo Reservation 33
school life 4. *See also* education issue
Seneca tribe 14
separatism 44
Shoshone Nation
    and land rights 70, 72, 73
Simmons, Gertrude 1–12
Sioux Indian Reservation 2
Sioux Indians 47
Sioux tribe 1, 4
    and Black Hills Council 9
Sisseton–Wahpeton reservations
    36
Six Nations 41
Six Nations Confederacy 14–15
Six Nations Defense League. *See*
    Indian Defense League of
    America

sixties culture 35–36
Snell bill 22
Society of American Indians
    (SAI) 8–9
star knowledge 45
state jurisdiction 22–23
The State of Native America 73
Sun Dance (opera) 8
Supreme Court
    and Indian fishing rights
        decision 41
    and land rights struggle 73

T

Tabbytite 26, 27
Taos Indians 25
Taos Pueblo 31
Tate'lyohiwin 2–3
Thorpe, Jim 57
Tigua Indians 38
Trail of Broken Treaties 51–52
    and Russell Means 60
Trail of Tears (painting) 89
trees, ceremonial 73–74
tribal conferences 45
tribal government 12, 31
tribalism 39
tribal power 38
tribal pride 51
tribal recognition 41
tribal sovereignty 93
tribal termination policy 88
tribal unity 2
Truman, President Harry 22
Tso, Mae Wilson **78–87**
    arrest of 83–84
Tuscarora people 14–15

U

Udall, Interior Secretary Stewart
    30
Udall, Morris 84–85
Uintah Reservation 7

Ute tribe 10

V

Vietnam War protest 32
violence 39
Voight, Jon 86

W

wampum belt return 41
water rights disputes 93
We Talk, You Listen 39
Where White Men Fear to Tread 61
Wilson, Richard
    and AIM 52
    election of 62
    opposition to 48
Winnebago land dispute 93
women leaders. *See also* Aquash,
    Anna Mae; Dann, Carrie; Harris,
    LaDonna; Simmons, Gertrude;
    Tso, Mae Wilson; *Women of the
    Native American Struggle*
    role in Indian culture 12
*Women of the Native American
    Struggle* 75
Wounded Knee confrontation 48,
    54
    and Anna Mae Aquash 67
    legal results of 55–56
    and Russell Means 61–62
    trials 42
Wounded Knee massacre 5

Y

Yankton Agency 2
Yellow Thunder, Raymond 51
    and NARF 92
Yowell, Chief Raymond 77

Z

Zitkala–Sa. *See* Simmons, Gertrude